Spring Quick Reference Guide

A Pocket Handbook for Spring Framework, Spring Boot, and More

Adam L. Davis

Apress®

Spring Quick Reference Guide: A Pocket Handbook for Spring Framework, Spring Boot, and More

Adam L. Davis
Oviedo, FL, USA

ISBN-13 (pbk): 978-1-4842-6143-9   ISBN-13 (electronic): 978-1-4842-6144-6
https://doi.org/10.1007/978-1-4842-6144-6

Copyright © 2020 by Adam L. Davis

Managing Director, Apress Media LLC: Welmoed Spahr
Acquisitions Editor: Steve Anglin
Development Editor: Matthew Moodie
Coordinating Editor: Mark Powers

Cover designed by eStudioCalamar

Cover image by Sergey Shmidt on Unsplash (www.unsplash.com)

Distributed to the book trade worldwide by Springer Science+Business Media, 1 New York Plaza, New York, NY 10004, U.S.A. Phone 1-800-SPRINGER, fax (201) 348-4505, e-mail orders-ny@ springer-sbm.com, or visit www.springeronline.com. Apress Media, LLC is a California LLC and the sole member (owner) is Springer Science + Business Media Finance Inc (SSBM Finance Inc). SSBM Finance Inc is a Delaware corporation.

For information on translations, please e-mail booktranslations@springernature.com; for reprint, paperback, or audio rights, please e-mail bookpermissions@springernature.com.

Apress titles may be purchased in bulk for academic, corporate, or promotional use. eBook versions and licenses are also available for most titles. For more information, reference our Print and eBook Bulk Sales web page at http://www.apress.com/bulk-sales.

Any source code or other supplementary material referenced by the author in this book is available to readers on GitHub via the book's product page, located at www.apress.com/9781484261439. For more detailed information, please visit http://www.apress.com/source-code.

Printed on acid-free paper

Dedicated to my sons
I hope your love of knowledge continues to flourish

Table of Contents

About the Author

Adam L. Davis makes software. He's spent many years developing in Java (since Java 1.2), has enjoyed using Spring for more than a decade, and is a Certified Spring Professional. He has experience using Java, Groovy, JavaScript, AWS, Hibernate, and much more to build applications and has worked at both large and small corporations.

Adam holds a master's degree in Computer Science from Georgia Tech. He is also the author of *Reactive Streams in Java* (Apress, 2019) and *Learning Groovy 3* (Apress, 2019). You can check out his website at http://adamldavis.com/.

About the Technical Reviewer

Manuel Jordan Elera is an autodidactic developer and researcher who enjoys learning new technologies for his own experiments and creating new integrations. Manuel won the Springy Award – Community Champion and Spring Champion 2013. In his little free time, he reads the Bible and composes music on his guitar. Manuel is known as dr_pompeii. He has tech-reviewed numerous books for Apress, including *Pro Spring Boot 2* (2019), *Rapid Java Persistence and Microservices* (2019), *Java Language Features* (2018), *Spring Boot 2 Recipes* (2018), and *Java APIs, Extensions and Libraries* (2018). Read his 13 detailed tutorials about many Spring technologies, contact him through his blog at www.manueljordanelera. blogspot.com, and follow him on his Twitter account, @dr_pompeii.

CHAPTER 1

Introduction

Spring has skyrocketed from a small open source project when it launched (version 1.0) in 2004 to an almost universal requirement of Java- and JVM-based projects today. What started as a more lightweight replacement for JEE has morphed into much more while still keeping to the fundamental principles.

Although some Spring subprojects, like *Spring Roo*, did not become extremely popular, many others have found an audience and flourished. There are a large number of projects under the "Spring" name, helping developers with everything from cloud applications to relational database queries and much more.

Note Every effort has been made to ensure that the information in this book is accurate, but due to the complexity of Spring and the many versions of Spring in the past and future, there may be some inaccuracies, such as new features that are not present at the time of writing, depending on which version you are using.

© Adam L. Davis 2020
A. L. Davis, *Spring Quick Reference Guide*, https://doi.org/10.1007/978-1-4842-6144-6_1

Who Should Read This Book

This book is for every Java developer that wants to know more about the Spring framework, Spring Boot, and related technologies. This book covers everything from the basics to some advanced topics. Not many words will be spent on the history; instead, it will focus on helpful information for developing applications right now.

Whether you're a beginner or a seasoned Java expert, this book should be useful.

About This Book

This book is organized so it might be read in order, for those who are new to Spring, or as a reference to come back to for many years into the future. Each chapter will cover a Spring project or core Spring framework and is divided into many titled sections. It will refer to all three ways to configure Spring Beans, XML, Java configuration classes, and component scanning, but with the main focus on the latter two.

This book will focus on core concepts and provide code samples. Examples will be practical and come from real-world experience.

Especially important information will be outlined as follows:

Tips   Text styled like this provides additional information that you may find very helpful.

Info   Text styled this way usually refers the curious reader to additional information located outside of this book.

Warnings   Text such as this cautions the wary reader to common problems that they might encounter.

Exercises   This is an exercise. We learn best by doing, so it's important that you try these out.

CHAPTER 2

Overview

Spring was initially started as an alternative to more heavy approaches to enterprise applications such as the J2EE standard. It made it possible to cleanly separate the framework from the code by allowing the configuration of *POJOs* (Plain Old Java Objects) rather than forcing classes to extend a certain class or implement an interface.

Spring grew and evolved over time and is the most popular Java framework for building applications today.

Core Spring

Core Spring includes Spring's Dependency Injection (DI) framework and configuration. The DI design pattern is a way to externalize the details of a dependency by allowing them to be injected. This, coupled with the use of interfaces, allows you to decouple code and makes software more manageable and extensible. DI is a subset of *Inversion of Control* (IoC), where the flow of an application is reversed or inverted.

Core Spring provides Spring containers, primarily implementations of the `BeanFactory` interface and its subinterface `ApplicationContext`. There are many implementations of `ApplicationContext`, and which one you use depends on the type of application. Most of the time, your application code need not be aware of the concrete type of the `BeanFactory` or `ApplicationContext`; it should only be defined once per application.

© Adam L. Davis 2020
A. L. Davis, *Spring Quick Reference Guide*, https://doi.org/10.1007/978-1-4842-6144-6_2

An ApplicationContext provides Bean factory methods for accessing application components (inherited from the `ListableBeanFactory interface`), the ability to load file resources in a generic fashion, the ability to publish events to registered listeners (inherited from the `ApplicationEventPublisher` interface), the ability to resolve messages supporting internationalization (inherited from the `MessageSource` interface), and possible inheritance from a parent ApplicationContext. ApplicationContext has many different subclasses, one of which is WebApplicationContext, which, as the same suggests, is useful for web applications.

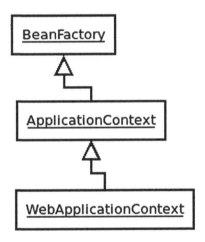

Figure 2-1. *Simplified class diagram for WebApplicationContext*

Beans from POJOs can be configured in one of three ways: XML, methods annotated with @Bean in a configuration Java class annotated with @Configuration, or when using component scanning, you can add an annotation such as @Component or @Service on the POJO class itself. The most recommended way is using one or more Java configuration classes for infrastructure and component scanning for business classes.

Spring Modules

Spring has many modules which can be included or not depending on the needs of the application. Here are some of the modules and projects under the Spring umbrella:

- Aspect-oriented programming (AOP) – Enables implementing cross-cutting concerns through runtime code interweaving.

- Spring Security – Authentication and authorization, configurable security that supports a range of standards, protocols, tools, and practices.

- Spring Data – Templates and tools for working with relational database management systems on the Java platform using Java Database Connectivity (JDBC), Object-Relational Mapping (ORM) tools, Reactive Relational Database Connectivity (R2DBC), and NoSQL databases.

- Core – Inversion of Control container, configuration of application components, and life-cycle management of Beans.

- Messaging – Registration of message listener objects for transparent message-consumption and sending to/from message queues via multiple transport layers including Java Message Service (JMS), AMQP, Kafka, and many others.

- Spring MVC (Model-View-Controller) – An HTTP and servlet-based framework providing hooks for extension and customization for web applications and RESTful (Representational State Transfer) web services.

- Transaction management – Unifies several transaction management APIs and coordinates transactions supporting JTA and JXA.

- Testing – Supports classes for writing both unit and integration tests such as Spring MVC Test which supports testing the controllers of Spring MVC applications.

- Spring Boot – Convention over configuration framework for simplifying application development. It includes auto-configuration and has "starter" dependencies that include many open source dependencies and the compatible versions of each dependency.

- Spring WebFlux – A reactive web framework using the reactive stream specification that can run on Netty, Tomcat, or Jetty (using Servlet 3.0 asynchronous threading).

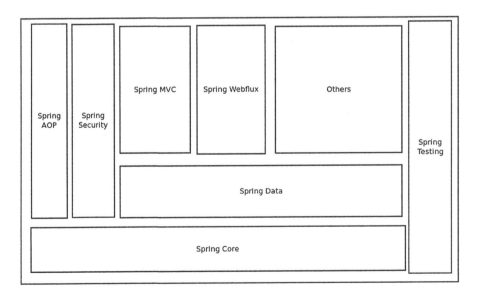

Figure 2-2. *Spring modules*

CHAPTER 3

Dependency Injection

Dependency Injection (DI) is at the heart of Spring. It refers to plugging in references at runtime between many different objects, either through a constructor, setter, or even directly to a field using runtime reflection. This enables IOC (Inversion of Control) where one class can use an instance of another class without knowing any details about how that object was constructed or its exact implementation class.

Spring's design allows the use of POJOs (Plain Old Java Objects). In other words, you don't need to implement a specific interface or extend a class in order to use Spring's DI. An instance of a class configured by Spring is called a *Spring Bean*, or sometimes just *bean* for short.

Decoupling

For example, you can annotate a setter or field with @Autowired on a Spring Bean, and Spring will find the class at runtime that best matches that field or setter. By default, it will search for the class matching the type. If it can't find a matching bean or there is more than one possible match (after considering any @Qualifier annotation and the name), Spring will throw an Exception and fail to start.

You should use interfaces to further decouple different classes. This way different components can be tested independently and not rely on the implementation of other components. Tight coupling in enterprise applications leads to brittle code and makes it very hard to make changes without breaking anything.

© Adam L. Davis 2020
A. L. Davis, *Spring Quick Reference Guide*, https://doi.org/10.1007/978-1-4842-6144-6_3

You can use @Qualifier to specify a specific name of an instance to help @Autowired find the right instance when many instances of the same class or interface might exist. We will show an example of this in the next section.

Configuration

Beans can be configured in one of three ways: XML, a configuration Java class annotated with @Configuration and methods annotated with @Bean, or on the Bean class itself with an annotation such as @Component. The most recommended way is using one or more Java configuration classes.

A configuration Java class annotated with @Configuration might look like the following:

```
@Configuration
public class Configuration {
  @Bean
  public MyService myService() {
    return new MyActualService();
  }
}
```

This configuration creates one bean instance of the Configuration class itself and one bean instance named myService of class MyActualService which implements the MyService interface (from the method annotated with @Bean).

Any configuration class must be nonfinal and nonlocal (public) and have a no-argument constructor. Spring proxies the class using CGLIB by default in order to enforce Spring bean dependency rules (which is why the class cannot be final). For example, this allows method calls to always return the singleton Bean instance instead of creating a new instance every time. If this behavior is not needed, you can supply proxyBeanMethods=false like the following:

```
@Configuration(proxyBeanMethods = false)
```

⚓ The default scope is "singleton," meaning one instance or "singleton" of the class will exist for the application. Other scopes such as "application," "request," and "session" exist in a web application. The "prototype" scope means a new instance will be created of the bean every time it's requested. A bean's scope can be changed using the @Scope annotation. For example, `@Scope("prototype")` `@Bean public MyService myService() {...}`

Every parameter to a method annotated with @Bean will be autowired by Spring (using the same rules that apply to @Autowired). For example, in the following configuration, the service2 bean will be wired to the myService bean:

Listing 3-1. Configuration.java

```
@Configuration
public class Configuration {
  @Bean
  public MyService myService() {
    return new MyActualService();
  }
  @Bean
  public OtherService service2(final MyService myService) {
    return new MyActualOtherService(myService);
  }
}
```

By default Spring uses the method name as the Bean's name. So the preceding example creates a Bean named "myService" and a Bean named "service2". You can override it by supplying a value to the @Bean annotation (like `@Bean("myname")`).

Using @Qualifier, the "service2" method could be rewritten as follows (with the same outcome):

```
@Bean
public OtherService service2(@Qualifier("myService")
MyService s) {
  return new MyActualOtherService(s);
}
```

In this way, even if multiple beans exist that implement MyService, Spring will know to choose the one named "myService".

ℹ You can also configure a bean to have multiple names. For example, using @Bean(name={"myname1", "myname2"}) would register the same bean under two names, myname1 and myname2.

Application Context

The ApplicationContext is the interface that directly exposes all of the beans configured by Spring.

It has a different concrete class depending on the type of application. For example, a web application will have an implementation of WebApplicationContext.

Component Scanning

You can use component scanning in Spring to scan classes for certain annotations on the class declaration. Those annotations are @Component, @Controller, @Service, and @Repository (and @Configuration). If they are found, Spring will initialize that POJO as a Spring Bean.

Component scanning can be configured through XML like the following:

```
<context:component-scan base-package="com.example"/>
```

or in a configuration class like this:

Listing 3-2. Configuration.java

```
@Configuration
@ComponentScan("com.example")
public class Configuration {
```

In these examples, the "com.example" package and all of its subpackages will be scanned for Spring annotations to create beans. Be careful not to scan too many classes as this will slow down initialization time.

Import

You can import other configuration files using @Import. Using @ComponentScan can also be used to scan for configuration classes (classes marked with @Configuration).

If you really need to, you can also use an @ImportResource annotation to load XML configuration files, for example:

```
@Import({WebConfig.class, ServiceConfig.class})
@ImportResource("dao.xml")
```

This would import the WebConfig and ServiceConfig configuration classes and the dao.xml Spring configuration file (see the next chapter for more about XML).

Laziness

Beans are created eagerly by default – which means Spring will instantiate them and wire them up at start-up time. This makes it faster to find any potential problems. You can make a Bean load lazily using the @Lazy annotation if you don't want it to load until necessary (when requested for using the ApplicationContext.getBean(String) method or requested by, e.g., autowiring).

Shut Down the ApplicationContext

In a web application, Spring already gracefully shuts down the ApplicationContext. However, in non-web applications, you need to register a shutdown hook.

Listing 3-3. App.java

```
public static void main(final String[] args) throws Exception {
  AbstractApplicationContext ctx
  = new ClassPathXmlApplicationContext(new String []
  {"beans.xml"});
  // add a shutdown hook for the above context...
  ctx.registerShutdownHook();
  // app runs here...
}
```

This way, Spring will gracefully shut down when the application exits.

BeanFactoryPostProcessors

The BeanFactoryPostProcessor interface can be implemented to change bean configurations before the beans are created (of all other beans). This can be useful for adding custom configuration, for example (although

Spring handles most useful cases by itself). The BeanFactoryPostProcessor interface has one method to define, postProcessBeanFactory (ConfigurableListableBeanFactory beanFactory). Spring automatically detects beans that implement this interface.

BeanPostProcessors

An ApplicationContext also automatically detects any beans that are defined in the configuration metadata it receives that implement the BeanPostProcessor interface. These beans are special because they are created at the same time as the ApplicationContext and before any other beans so they can process other bean definitions.

The org.springframework.beans.factory.config.BeanPostProcessor interface consists of exactly two callback methods:

```
Object postProcessBeforeInitialization(Object bean, String
beanName)
   throws BeansException
```

```
Object postProcessAfterInitialization(Object bean, String
beanName)
   throws BeansException
```

Q Spring AOP, which we will cover later, is implemented using the BeanPostProcessor interface. It can replace each bean with a proxy of that bean.

Init and Destroy Methods

You can enable JSR-250 annotations like @PostConstruct and @PreDestroy using the CommonAnnotationBeanPostProcessor in Spring. It's activated by component scanning but otherwise can be activated directly in your Spring configuration.

An alternative is to use Spring's built-in configuration. For example, the Bean annotation, @Bean(initMethod = "up", destroyMethod = "down") would cause Spring to call "up" after initializing the class and injecting all dependencies and "down" right before destroying it.

Properties

By default, Spring Boot will load properties from your classpath from a file named application.properties (for standard properties) or application.yml (for YAML-formatted properties).

Additional properties can be loaded into the environment using the @PropertySource annotation.

For example, the following loads a property file named app.properties from the classpath under the /com/acme/ directory:

Listing 3-4. AppConfig.java

```
@Configuration
@PropertySource("classpath:/com/acme/app.properties")
public class AppConfig {
  //configuration code...
}
```

You can then use properties from the environment and inject them using the @Value annotation:

```
@Value("${bean.name}") String beanName;
@Bean
public MyBean myBean() {
  return new MyBean(beanName);
}
```

The file named app.properties could have the following value:

```
bean.name=Bob
```

This would inject "Bob" into the beanName field previously mentioned.

Environment

An alternative to using the @Value annotation is to use the `org.spring framework.core.env.Environment` class. It can be autowired into any class (using, e.g., @Autowired). It has the following methods for getting access to defined properties at runtime:

- String getProperty(String key) – Gets the value for a given property key or null if not resolved

- String getProperty(String key, String defaultValue) – Gets the value for a given property key or the given defaultValue if not found

- String getRequiredProperty(String key) – Gets the value for a given property key or throws an IllegalStateException if not found

Profiles

Spring Profiles allow you to configure different properties and even Beans to be initialized at runtime depending on the active Profile(s). They can be useful when deploying the same application to different environments, such as "Staging," "Test," and "Production." You can have any number of profiles with any names.

You can set the current Profile or Profiles active using the `spring. profiles.active` system property or spring_profiles_active environment variable. You can have as many profiles active as you want (separate them using commas).

The `@Profile` annotation can annotate a `@Component` bean class (or the stereotype annotations, `@Service, @Repository`, and `@Controller`) or a `@Bean` annotated method or even a `@Configuration` annotated configuration class.

For example, the following configuration class defines two different databases. Which one is active is dependent on the profile active.

Listing 3-5. ProfileDatabaseConfig.java

```
@Configuration
public class ProfileDatabaseConfig {

  @Bean("dataSource")
  @Profile("development")
  public DataSource embeddedDatabase() { ... }

  @Bean("dataSource")
  @Profile("production")
  public DataSource productionDatabase() { ... }
}
```

⚠ Make sure you use a different name for each @Bean method in a Configuration class even when those beans are marked for different profiles. Otherwise, you could get unexpected behavior from Spring since it uses the method names for the bean names.

SpEL

What is Spring Expression Language (SpEL)? The Spring Expression Language (SpEL for short) is a powerful expression language that supports querying and manipulating an object graph at runtime.

SpEL can be injected using the @Value annotation with the #{} syntax. Unlike using ${}, which only is interpreted as environment properties, using #{} allows you to use the full expressiveness of an embedded language (SpEL).

```
@Value("#{ T(java.lang.Math).random() * 100.0 }")
int randomNumber;
```

The **T** syntax is used to refer to a Java type (the preceding java.lang. Math class).

You can also refer to system properties using the built-in variable systemProperties:

```
@Value("#{ systemProperties['user.region'] }")
String region;
```

SpEL also has the Elvis operator and the safe navigator (much like in Kotlin, Groovy, and other languages), for example:

```
@Value("#{systemProperties['pop3.port'] ?: 25}")
```

This would default to 25 if no value was given for pop3.port.

You can also specify String literals using single quotes, for example:

```
@Value("#{ 'Hello '.concat('World!') }")
String hello;
```

It would result in hello having the value "Hello World!".

SpEL is also useful for *Spring Security* annotations which we will cover in a subsequent chapter.

Testing

Spring provides testing support as part of spring-test. For a JUnit 4 test, you can specify how the ApplicationContext should be created for JUnit unit or integration tests using Spring's SpringRunner and the @ContextConfiguration annotation, for example:

Listing 3-6. MyTest.java

```
@RunWith(SpringRunner.class)
// ApplicationContext will be loaded from AppConfig and
TestConfig
@ContextConfiguration(classes = {AppConfig.class, TestConfig.
class})
public class MyTest {
// class body...
}
```

A JUnit 5 test is similar but uses @ExtendWith(SpringExtension. class) instead of @RunWith:

Listing 3-7. MyTest5.java

```
import org.junit.jupiter.api.Test;
import org.junit.jupiter.api.extension.ExtendWith;
import org.springframework.test.context.junit.jupiter.
SpringExtension;

@ExtendWith(SpringExtension.class)
@ContextConfiguration(classes = {AppConfig.class, TestConfig.
class})
public class MyTest5 {
// class body...
}
```

✎ Write a Spring application including a JUnit test.

CHAPTER 4

XML Configuration

Spring configuration can be done through XML. In fact, this was the only way to configure Spring beans before Java configuration was introduced. We will cover some Spring XML for reference material and for use in legacy applications.

XML

The XML standard is composed of the basic syntax, namespaces, and XML schema definitions. The syntax, in a nutshell, is based around Elements, names, typically lowercase, surrounded by greater-than and less-than symbols (like <bean>); attributes which can be set within those symbols and use double quotes (like <bean name="myBean">); and elements can be nested, where the nesting is ended with a backslash (like </beans>).

For clarification, let's look at the first three lines typically found in any Spring configuration XML file and break down what they mean:

```
<?xml version="1.0" encoding="UTF-8"?>
<beans xmlns="http://www.springframework.org/schema/beans"
       xmlns:xsi="http://www.w3.org/2001/XMLSchema-instance"
```

1. <?xml... declares this is an XML file.

2. <beans is the root element (the one element that
    wraps the entire document), and xmlns="..." declares
    the root namespace. This allows you to reference
    <bean> without specifying a namespace, for
    example.

3. xmlns:xsi= declares the "xsi" namespace
    which stands for XML Schema Instance. This
    allows the document to subsequently use
    xsi:schemaLocation= to define where to locate the
    corresponding XML schemas.

Spring XML Configuration Organization

To keep things organized and easier to understand, it makes sense in a
medium- to large-sized application to use multiple XML files and split up
the configuration among them. You can decide to segregate the files in
many different ways: horizontal slices (controls, services, and repositories
or DAOs (Data Access Objects)), vertical slices (by feature), or by function
(web services, front end, and back end).

XML Application Context

To get started, use one of the following application contexts:

- ClassPathXmlApplicationContext

- FileSystemXmlApplicationContext

- XmlWebApplicationContext

For both ClassPathXmlApplicationContext and FileSystemXml
ApplicationContext, you need to specify the XML file or files.

Classpath

For example, here is an application entry class, App, that uses a
ClassPathXmlApplicationContext:

Listing 4-1. App.java

```
package com.apress.spring_quick.di;

import com.apress.spring_quick.config.AppSpringConfig;
import com.apress.spring_quick.di.model.Message;
import org.springframework.context.ApplicationContext;
import org.springframework.context.support.
ClassPathXmlApplicationContext;

public class App {

    public static void main(String[] args) {
        final ApplicationContext applicationContext =
          new ClassPathXmlApplicationContext("classpath:/
          application.xml");
        final MyBeanInterface myBean = applicationContext
            .getBean(MyBeanInterface.class);
        //...
    }
}
```

In this example, "classpath:/application.xml" refers to a file named
application.xml at the root of the classpath (typically included in, e.g.,
a JAR file). In a typical build, you should put this file in the src/main/
resources/ directory, and Maven or Gradle will add it to the JAR file
automatically during the build. Although here we supply one file, multiple
XML files could be used.

Web

For XmlWebApplicationContext, the default location for the root context (the application context which could be the parent of multiple servlet contexts) is "/WEB-INF/applicationContext.xml", and "/WEB-INF/<name>-servlet.xml" for a context with the namespace "<name>-servlet". For example, with a DispatcherServlet instance with the servlet-name "products", it would look for "/WEB-INF/products-servlet.xml".

XML Beans

The most basic thing to do in Spring XML is to create beans. Here is an example of how the application.xml file might look:

Listing 4-2. application.xml

```
<?xml version="1.0" encoding="UTF-8"?>
<beans xmlns="http://www.springframework.org/schema/beans"
       xmlns:xsi="http://www.w3.org/2001/XMLSchema-instance"
       xsi:schemaLocation="http://www.springframework.org/
       schema/beans
       http://www.springframework.org/schema/beans/spring-
       beans.xsd">
    <bean class=
"org.springframework.beans.factory.config.
PropertyPlaceholderConfigurer">
        <property name="locations"
             value="classpath:db/datasource.properties"/>
    </bean>
    <bean id="dataSource1"
      class="org.springframework.jdbc.datasource.
      DriverManagerDataSource">
```

```
    <property name="driverClassName" value="${db.driver
    ClassName}"/>
    <property name="url" value="${db.url}"/>
    <property name="username" value="${db.username}"/>
    <property name="password" value="${db.password}"/>
  </bean>
</beans>
```

This example shows how to define Spring beans and set properties on those beans. Note that you can reference properties using the ${} syntax, such as how ${db.driverClassName} references the db.driverClassName property.

Init and Destroy

The initialize method (which is called right after Spring has instantiated and resolved all dependencies on a bean) can be configured by setting the init-method attribute on a bean definition, as shown in the following XML configuration:

```
<bean name="userService"
  class="com.apress.spring_quick.service.UserService"
  init-method="doInitialization" />
```

The destroy method (which is called right before Spring discards a Spring bean) can be configured by setting the destroy-method attribute as seen in the following XML configuration:

```
<bean name="userService"
  class="com.apress.spring_quick.service.UserService"
  destroy-method="doCleanup" />
```

This can be used to remove any resources that are not needed anymore when the bean is destroyed. This would call a method defined like the following:

```
public void doCleanup() {
 // do clean up
}
```

Both the init-method and destroy-method should be public and have void as the return type.

Enabling AOP

In XML, use `<aop:aspectj-autoproxy>` in the same application context as the object to apply the aspect to (in particular, in a typical Spring Web MVC application applicationContext.xml and `...-servlet.xml`).

AOP Configuration

The following example XML configuration uses Spring AOP and the Spring Retry[1] project to repeat a service call to a method called `remoteCall` in any class or interface ending with "Service":

```
<?xml version = "1.0" encoding = "UTF-8"?>
<beans xmlns = "http://www.springframework.org/schema/beans"
   xmlns:xsi = "http://www.w3.org/2001/XMLSchema-instance"
   xmlns:aop = "http://www.springframework.org/schema/aop"
   xsi:schemaLocation = "http://www.springframework.org/
   schema/beans
```

---

[1]https://github.com/spring-projects/spring-retry

```
http://www.springframework.org/schema/beans/spring-beans.xsd
http://www.springframework.org/schema/aop
http://www.springframework.org/schema/aop/spring-aop.xsd">

<aop:config>
    <aop:pointcut id="remote"
        expression="execution(* com..*Service.remoteCall(..))" />
    <aop:advisor pointcut-ref="remote"
        advice-ref="retryAdvice" />
</aop:config>

<bean id="retryAdvice"
class="org.springframework.retry.interceptor.
RetryOperationsInterceptor"
/>
<!-- other bean definitions... -->

</beans>
```

Note that the pointcut-ref references the previously defined pointcut named "remote". Please see Chapter 5 for more details.

Enabling Spring Data JPA

Spring Data JPA allows you to interact with a database using an ORM (Object-Relational Mapping) such as Hibernate or EclipseLink. To enable Spring Data JPA in XML, use the following XML:

```
<beans xmlns="http://www.springframework.org/schema/beans"
    xmlns:xsi="http://www.w3.org/2001/XMLSchema-instance"
    xmlns:jpa="http://www.springframework.org/schema/data/jpa"
    xsi:schemaLocation="http://www.springframework.org/schema/beans
```

```
https://www.springframework.org/schema/beans/spring-beans.xsd
http://www.springframework.org/schema/data/jpa
https://www.springframework.org/schema/data/jpa/spring-jpa.xsd">

 <jpa:repositories base-package="com.acme.repositories"/>
</beans>
```

This would scan the "com.acme.repositories" package and below for any JPA repositories. See Chapter 6 for more information.

Mixing XML and Java Configuration

There's no reason you can't use a mix of XML configuration and Java configuration. In fact, you can activate Java configuration from XML and import an XML configuration file from Java.

For example, the following Spring XML file enables Java configuration:

```
<?xml version="1.0" encoding="UTF-8"?>
<beans xmlns="http://www.springframework.org/schema/beans"
      xmlns:xsi="http://www.w3.org/2001/XMLSchema-instance"
      xmlns:context="http://www.springframework.org/schema/
      context"
      xsi:schemaLocation="http://www.springframework.org/
      schema/beans
       http://www.springframework.org/schema/beans/spring-
       beans.xsd
       http://www.springframework.org/schema/context
       http://www.springframework.org/schema/context/spring-
       context.xsd">

 <context:component-scan base-package="com.apress.spring.
 config" />

</beans>
```

This XML starts a component scan in the "com.apress.spring. config" package and any subpackages. Any files marked with @Configuration, @Component, or many other annotations would be picked up by Spring.

From a Spring Java configuration file, you can use @ImportResource to import Spring XML files, for example:

```
@Configuration
@ImportResource( { "spring-context1.xml", "spring-context2.xml" } )
public class ConfigClass { }
```

If enabled as configuration in a Spring application (either through component scanning or other means), this class would make Spring read both files, "spring-context1.xml" and "spring-context2.xml", as Spring XML configuration.

✏️EXERCISE: USE BOTH XML AND JAVA CONFIG

Create a new application and use both Spring XML and Spring Java configuration. Experiment in how they can be combined in different ways.

CHAPTER 5

Spring AOP

AOP stands for aspect-oriented programming. AOP allows you to address cross-cutting concerns, such as logging, transaction management, security, and caching, without repeating the same code over and over. It allows you to apply the DRY (Do not Repeat Yourself) principle.

Spring uses AOP itself in many ways, but also directly exposes the tooling to developers.

In short, you use Spring AOP by defining a pointcut (where to add additional features) and advice (the feature you are adding).

Spring creates two types of proxies, either JDK[1] (when implementing an interface, this is built-in to the JDK) or CGLIB[2] (when manipulating bytecode which is necessary when there is not an interface). Final classes or methods cannot be proxied since they cannot be extended. Also, due to the proxy implementation, Spring AOP only applies to public, nonstatic methods on Spring Beans.

---

[1]https://docs.oracle.com/javase/8/docs/technotes/guides/reflection/proxy.html
[2]https://github.com/cglib/cglib

© Adam L. Davis 2020
A. L. Davis, *Spring Quick Reference Guide*, https://doi.org/10.1007/978-1-4842-6144-6_5

Terminology

Spring AOP uses the following terms:

- Aspect – The modularization of concerns that act as cross-cutting concerns.

- Join point – It is a point during the execution of the method.

- Advice – The action taken by an aspect at the join point.

- Pointcut – The predicate that matches one or more join points is called a pointcut.

- Weaving – The process of adding advice to a pointcut.

- Introduction – Defining additional method fields for a type.

- Target object – Those objects which are advised by aspects are target objects.

- AOP proxy – The object created by Spring AOP to meet an aspect contract. It executes the advice where it should be applied and delegates to the object being proxied (the target object).

Advice

There are five types of advice (each with corresponding annotation):

1. Before – Runs before a method execution

2. After – Always runs after a method execution, regardless of result (similar to `finally` keyword in Java)

3. AfterThrowing – Only runs when a method throws an exception

4. AfterReturning – Only runs when a method returns a value and can use that value

5. Around – Wraps around the method execution and is given a single argument of type `ProceedingJoinPoint` which you must call `proceed()` on to actually invoke the wrapped method

How to Enable AOP

You can enable Spring AOP using the `@EnableAspectJAutoProxy` annotation on a configuration.

```
@Configuration
@EnableAspectJAutoProxy
public class AppConfig {
}
```

Each Aspect class should be annotated with `@Aspect` annotation. Within that class, you then specify Pointcuts and Advice. It should also be annotated with `@Component` to be picked up by annotation scanning (or configured as a Spring bean in another way).

How to Define a Pointcut

You define a pointcut using a *pointcut expression* (a subset of expressions defined by the AspectJ project). Within an Aspect using annotations, you use the @Pointcut annotation on an empty method, and the name of the pointcut is the method's name, for example:

```
@Pointcut("execution(* save(..))")
private void dataSave() {}
```

Here, the name of the pointcut is "dataSave()". A Pointcut method's return type must be void. It can be of any visibility.

In this example, the pointcut is execution(* save(..)) which refers to execution of any method named save on any class. The first * is a wildcard (matching everything) and refers to the return type of the method. The .. refers to the method parameters and means "zero to many parameters," while "save" is the method name. The Pointcut method itself (dataSave) does not need any code. Use a Pointcut by annotating another method using the name of the pointcut, for example, assuming the save methods return a value or throw an Exception:

Listing 5-1. Advice examples

```
@AfterReturning(value = "dataSave()", returning = "entity")
public void logSave(JoinPoint jp, Object entity) throws
Throwable {
  // log the entity here
}
@AfterThrowing(pointcut = "dataSave()", throwing = "ex")
public void doAfterThrowing(Exception ex) {
  // you can intercept thrown exception here.
}
@Around("execution(* save(..))")
```

```
public Object aroundSave(ProceedingJoinPoint jp) throws
Throwable {
  return jp.proceed();
}
```

As shown in the preceding method, the `aroundSave` advice can declare pointcut expressions directly as well.

The Pointcut expression in Spring AOP can use keywords `execution` and `within` as well as &&, ||, and ! (and, or, not). Here are some more examples:

Listing 5-2. Pointcut examples

```
@Pointcut("execution(public * *(..))")
private void anyPublicOperation() {}

@Pointcut("within(com.xyz..*)")
private void inXyz() {}

@Pointcut("anyPublicOperation() && inXyz()")
private void xyzOperation() {}
```

The `anyPublicOperation` pointcut refers to every public method.

The `inXyz` pointcut refers to every method of every class in the com.xyz package.

The **xyzOperation** pointcut combines both of the other two pointcuts, meaning every public method within the com.xyz package.

Annotations

You can also specify annotations within pointcut expressions using either @target, @annotation, or annotations directly, for example:

```
@Pointcut("@target(org.springframework.stereotype.Repository)")
public void allRepositories() {}
// use an annotation on each actual method to advise:
@Pointcut("@annotation(com.apress.spring_quick.aop.LogMe)")
public void logMes() {}
```

In the preceding example, the first pointcut applies to target classes annotated with @Repository, and the second pointcut refers to methods annotated with @LogMe. You can also use @args to specify that an argument of the method has a specific annotation.

Pointcut Expressions

There are many keywords supported by Spring AOP pointcut expressions. Although some of these expressions match identical join points in Spring AOP, they can be used for different bindings (which we will cover next). For reference, here are many of the possible expressions:

execution(public * *(..))	Every public method.
execution(* set*(..))	Every method with a name starting with "set".
execution(* com.xyz.service. AccountService.*(..))	Every method defined in the AccountService interface.
execution(* com.xyz. service.*.*(..))	Every nonprivate method defined in every class or interface in the "com.xyz.service" package.

(continued)

execution(* com.xyz. service..*.*(..))	Every nonprivate method defined in every class or interface in the "com.xyz.service" package and subpackages.
within(com.xyz.service.*)	Every join point with the "com.xyz.service" package.
within(com.xyz.service..*)	Every join point with the "com.xyz.service" package and subpackages.
this(com.xyz.service. AccountService)	Every join point where the proxy implements the com.xyz.service.AccountService interface.
target(com.xyz.service. AccountService)	Every join point where the target object implements the com.xyz.service.AccountService interface.
args(java.io.Serializable)	Any method that has one argument at runtime whose type is java.io.Serializable.
@target(org.springframework. transaction.annotation. Transactional)	Any join point where the target object is annotated with @Transactional.
@within(org.springframework. transaction.annotation. Transactional)	Any join point where the declared type of the target object is annotated with @Transactional.
@annotation(org. springframework.transaction. annotation.Transactional)	Any method which is annotated with @Transactional.
@args(com.xyz.security. MyAnnotation)	Any method with a single argument annotated with com.xyz.security.MyAnnotation.
execution(@com.xyz.security. LogMe void *(..))	Any method annotated with @com.xyz.security. LogMe and has a void return type.

Bindings in Spring AOP

Any advice method may declare as its first parameter a parameter of type org.aspectj.lang.JoinPoint (please note that around advice is *required* to declare a first parameter of type ProceedingJoinPoint, which is a subinterface of JoinPoint). The JoinPoint interface provides a number of useful methods such as the following:

getArgs()	Returns the method arguments.
getThis()	Returns the proxy object.
getSignature()	Returns a description of the method that is being advised.
toString()	Returns a useful description of the method being advised.
getTarget()	Returns the target object.

You can also pass in parameters to advice using the pointcut expression to link arguments using the args, this, @annotation, or other keywords, for example:

```
@Before("dataSave() && args(course,..)")
public void validateCourse(Course course) {
    // ...
}
```

This serves two purposes: it validates that the first argument is of type Course, and it provides that argument to the advice method.

Limitations of Spring AOP

Spring AOP can only advise public, nonstatic methods on Spring Beans.

There are some limitations of weaving with proxies. For example, if there is an internal method call from one method to another within the same class, the advice will never be executed for the internal method call. See the figure, "Spring AOP proxy," for an illustration of this concept.

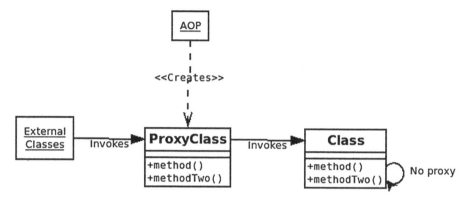

Figure 5-1. *Spring AOP proxy*

In this illustration, when method() calls methodTwo() internal to Class, it never invokes the ProxyClass so no AOP Advice is invoked. However, any external classes (other Spring beans) will invoke the proxy methods which apply any before, after, or around logic.

Alternatives

If you need additional functionality, you could use AspectJ directly. Additionally, projects like Lombok[3] provide bytecode manipulation for different purposes, such as creating immutable data classes, which we will explore in subsequent chapters.

---

[3]https://projectlombok.org/

CHAPTER 6

Spring Data

Spring Data's mission is to provide a familiar and consistent Spring-based programming model for data access while still retaining the special traits of the underlying data store.

Spring Data has support for every kind of data store, both relational and nonrelational (SQL and NoSQL), from JPA (Hibernate or TopLink) to Apache Cassandra and MongoDB to Redis. In this chapter, we will explore Spring Data JPA, JDBC, and R2DBC and how they support relational databases such as MariaDB, Oracle, or PostgreSQL.

Domain Entities

To get started in any Spring Data project, we need to define the domain classes or entities that our project depends upon. These are the domain objects that map to our database tables and are highly dependent upon the business domain of the application.

Spring Data integrates well with the standard annotations under the "javax.persistence" package. For this chapter, assume a Customer entity class defined like the following:

```
import javax.persistence.*;
import lombok.*;
```

© Adam L. Davis 2020
A. L. Davis, *Spring Quick Reference Guide*, https://doi.org/10.1007/978-1-4842-6144-6_6

```
@Data
@Entity
@RequiredArgsConstructor
@Table("customers")
public class Customer {

  private @GeneratedValue @Id Long id;
  private final String firstname;
  @Column("surname")
  private final String lastname;

}
```

The @Entity annotation is necessary to mark this class for Spring Data as an entity class. The @Id annotation marks the field representing the primary key of the table. Optional annotations like @Table and @Column can be used to use names which do not match the class of field names, respectively. Note that we are using Lombok's @Data and @RequiredArgsConstructor to remove the need for repetitive code such as getters, setters, toString, equals, hashCode, and constructors. In this case, since firstname and lastname are final, @RequiredArgsConstructor creates a constructor that sets those two values from two parameters.

Also, we will be using the following Course class:

Listing 6-1. Course.java

```
import org.springframework.data.jpa.domain.AbstractPersistable;
import javax.persistence.Column;
import javax.persistence.Entity;
import javax.persistence.NamedQuery;
```

```
@Entity
@NamedQuery(name = "Course.findByTheName",
    query = "from Course c where c.name = ?1")
public class Course extends AbstractPersistable<Long> {

    @Column(unique = true)
    private String name;
    private String subtitle;
    private String description;

    public Course() { this(null); }

    public Course(Long id) {
        this.setId(id);
    }
  // getters and setters omitted
}
```

Note that we use @NamedQuery here to define a custom query directly
on the entity class. We also are using @Column(unique = true)
to specify that the name column is unique. Also, by extending Abstract
Persistable<Long>, we inherit an Id property with a type of Long and
denote this class as a database persistable entity to Spring Data. This is
optional.

Course and Customer are deliberately defined in a different way
to demonstrate some of the possible ways to define domain entities in
Spring Data.

This book will refer back frequently to the domain of an online
learning application that has Courses and Customers.

Spring Data JDBC

Spring Data JDBC is similar to Spring Data JPA, building upon many of the same abstractions, except Spring Data JDBC

- Has no lazy loading

- Has no caching built-in

- Is more simple

- Uses the concept of Aggregate Root

- Supports defining a query manually only as a String in a @Query annotation, not through a method name

An Aggregate Root is a Root entity that when you save, it saves all of its references as well, and upon editing all of its references will be deleted and reinserted.

Getting Started

To get started, include the spring-data-jdbc jar dependency in your project.

In a Maven project, put the following under dependencies:

```
<dependency>
  <groupId>org.springframework.data</groupId>
  <artifactId>spring-data-jdbc</artifactId>
  <version>2.0.1.RELEASE</version>
</dependency>
```

Or in a Gradle build, include the following under dependencies:

```
implementation 'org.springframework.data:spring-data-
jdbc:2.0.1.RELEASE'
```

Use the @EnableJdbcRepositories annotation to enable them using Java configuration, for example, using a Java configuration class named CategoryConfiguration:

```
@Configuration
@EnableJdbcRepositories
public class CategoryConfiguration {}
```

Defining a Repository

CRUD stands for "Create, Read, Update, Delete." In Spring Data, the CrudRepository<T,ID> interface provides built-in methods for interacting with a persistent data store, such as a relational database.

To define your repository, create an interface and extend CrudRepository<T,ID> with the generic types defined where T is the type of your entity class and ID is the type of its identifier. Spring will automatically implement the repository for you, including the following methods (this is not an exhaustive list):

- S save(S entity) – Saves the entity to the database
- findAll() – Returns all of them
- S findById(ID)
- count()
- delete(T)
- existsById(ID)

Custom Queries

When either using Spring Data JDBC and you need custom queries or using Spring Data JPA and the built-in Spring Data conventions do not suffice, you can specify custom SQL (or JPQL when using Spring Data JPA) queries using the @Query annotation, for example:

```
@Query("SELECT * FROM customer WHERE lastname = :lastname")
List<Customer> findAllByLastname(@Param("lastname") String
lastname);

@Query("SELECT firstname, lastname FROM Customer WHERE
lastname = ?1")
Customer findFirstByLastname(String lastname);
```

The findAllByLastname query would find all Customer entities by lastname. Spring Data JDBC only supports named params (like the preceding :lastname), whereas Spring Data JPA also supports indexed parameters (like the preceding ?1). The @Param annotation tells Spring Data the name of the query parameter.

ⓘ Spring supports Java 8 and above parameter name discovery based on the -parameters compiler flag. By using this flag in your build (which Spring Boot handles for you), you can omit the @Param annotation for named parameters.

You can also define modifying statements such as the following:

```
@Query("delete from Customer c where c.active = false")
void deleteInactiveCustomers();
```

Custom Queries in JPA

You can also define method signatures using a basic syntax, and Spring will implement them within Spring Data JPA. Examples are as follows:

- findByX – Finds one entity by a given value or values; X is a condition (we will cover what types of conditions are allowed).

- findByFirstname(String name) – In this example, Firstname is the property by which to search.

- findByFirstnameAndLastname – You can use "And", "Or", and "Not".

- OrderByY – Orders by "Y" property.

- findAllByX – Finds all records that match a condition.

- countByX – Counts all the records that match a condition.

- findTopN – Returns only the top N records.

Conditions

The following are examples of conditions allowed in custom query method expressions:

- `Name(String name)`, `NameEquals(String name)`, `NameIs(String name)` – Is or Equals are supported but are also implied by default.

- `IdGreaterThan(Long num)` – Where id is greater than the given num.

- `IdLessThan(Long num)` – Where id is less than the given num.

- `DateLessThan(Date d)` – Where date is less than the given date, d.

- `DateGreaterThan(Date d)` – Where date is greater than the given date, d.

- `DateBetween(Date d1, Date d2)` – Where date is greater than or equal to d1 and less than or equal to d2.

- `DateBefore(Date d), DateAfter(Date d)` – Works similar to LessThan and GreaterThan but only for dates.

- `NameLike(String string)` – Where name is like the given value, string.

- `NameStartingWith(String string)` – Where name starts with the given value, string.

- `NameEndingWith(String string)` – Where name ends with the given value, string.

- `NameContaining(String string)` – Where name contains the given String.

- `NameIgnoreCase(String string)` – Where the name equals the given value ignoring the case (case-insensitive matching).

- `AgeIn(Collection<Long> ages)` – Where age matches any value in a given collection.

- `AgeNotIn(Collection<Long> ages)` – Where age does not match any value in a given collection.

JdbcTemplate

For a more direct connection to a database, you can use `org.springframework.jdbc.core.JdbcTemplate<T>`.

- `void query(String sql, Object[] args, RowCallbackHandler rch)` – This method takes an SQL query, any number of arguments as an Object array, and a callback that gets called for each row of results.

- `<T> List<T> query(String sql, Object[] args, RowMapper<T> rowMapper)` – This method is the same as the previous except it takes a RowMapper<T> which converts rows into POJOs and returns a List of those POJOs.

Spring Data JPA

You can enable Spring Data repository proxy creation via Java or XML, for example:

Listing 6-2. DataConfig.java

```
import org.springframework.data.jpa.repository.config.
EnableJpaRepositories;

@EnableJpaRepositories
@Configuration
class DataConfig { //... }
```

Spring will then automatically create proxy instances of all declared Repository interfaces at runtime (under the package of the DataConfig class). The preceding @EnableJpaRepositories annotation will enable JPA; there are also other flavors like @EnableMongoRepositories.

To enable in Spring Data JPA in XML:

```
<beans xmlns="http://www.springframework.org/schema/beans"
  xmlns:xsi="http://www.w3.org/2001/XMLSchema-instance"
  xmlns:jpa="http://www.springframework.org/schema/data/jpa"
  xsi:schemaLocation="http://www.springframework.org/schema/beans
    https://www.springframework.org/schema/beans/spring-beans.xsd
    http://www.springframework.org/schema/data/jpa
    https://www.springframework.org/schema/data/jpa/spring-jpa.xsd">

  <jpa:repositories base-package="com.acme.repositories"/>
</beans>
```

Paging and Sorting

You can create a Repository interface and extend CrudRepository<T,ID>, and Spring will generate implementations to the built-in method from CrudRepository<T,ID> for you as well as custom query methods that you define using Spring Data's naming conventions.

For example, the following interface extends CrudRepository<T,ID> and adds a method for finding Customer entities by *lastName*:

Listing 6-3. PersonRepository.java

```
@Repository
public interface PersonRepository extends
CrudRepository<Customer, Long> {
  List<Customer> findByLastname(String lastname);
  // additional custom query methods go here
}
```

Using the @Repository annotation here is not necessary, but you may want to add it to remind everyone that this interface is proxied and the proxy exists as a Spring bean.

On top of the CrudRepository<T,ID>, there is a PagingAndSortin gRepository<T,ID> abstraction that adds additional methods to ease paginated access to entities. It looks like the following:

```
public interface PagingAndSortingRepository<T, ID>
        extends CrudRepository<T, ID> {
  Iterable<T> findAll(Sort sort);
  Page<T> findAll(Pageable pageable);
}
```

You can also add Sort or Pageable parameters to custom methods to achieve sorting and pagination of results.

Transactions

Transactions are atomic units of work – typically on a database – that either complete fully or are rolled back (canceled) completely if something fails and can contain any number of statements. Spring can assist in handling transactions either programmatically or through annotation processing – with the latter being preferred.

To begin, make sure to include the required dependencies to your project and then enable Spring's Transaction annotation processing. Note that in XML you would use <tx:annotation-driven/> or in Java use @EnableTransactionManagement to get annotation-based configuration working.

Then you can annotate a method (or class) with @Transactional. When annotating a class, all methods of that class will inherit those transaction settings. It will wrap each method in a Transaction using Spring's proxy of your class.

⚠️ Another consequence of using proxies is that methods are only wrapped in a Transaction when called externally. In other words, if one method of a class directly calls another method in the same class that has @Transactional on it, it will not invoke the proxy, and thus the Transaction will not be initiated (or handled according to the annotation settings).

You can also annotate an interface to have every method affected; however, this is not suggested by the Spring team since it will only work if the proxy directly implements the interface.

Transactions can be given timeouts measured in seconds. They can also be marked as "read only" and have different isolation levels, propagation settings, and other different transaction settings.

For example, here is an annotated method definition of a query:

```
@Transactional(timeout = 10, readOnly = true,
    propagation = Propagation.REQUIRES_NEW)
Customer findByBirthdateAndLastname(LocalDate date, String
lastname);
```

This would have a timeout of ten seconds. The readOnly qualifier gives a hint to the JDBC driver and might improve performance, but the behavior depends on the driver. The propagation is set to REQUIRES_NEW which is explained next.

🔍 Transactions are only rolled back for *unchecked* Exceptions by default. You can change this by setting the rollbackFor property of the @Transactional annotation.

The different propagation settings available are as follows:

- REQUIRED – To either join an active transaction or to start a new one if the method gets called without a transaction (this is the default behavior).

- SUPPORTS – To join an active transaction if one exists, otherwise without a transactional context.

- MANDATORY – To join an active transaction if one exists or to throw an Exception if the method gets called without an active transaction.

- NEVER – To throw an Exception if the method gets called in the context of an active transaction.

- NOT_SUPPORTED – To suspend an active transaction (if one exists) and to execute the method without any transactional context.

- REQUIRES_NEW – To always start a new transaction for this method. If the method gets called with an active transaction, that transaction is suspended, while this method is executed.

- NESTED – To start a new transaction if the method gets called without an active transaction, and if it gets called with an active transaction, a new transaction is created that wraps only this method execution.

You can also set the isolation level of a Transaction to one of five different values (using, e.g., @Transaction(isolation = Isolation. READ_COMMITTED)):

- DEFAULT – This is the default and depends on what the default isolation level is for your database.

- READ_UNCOMMITTED – This is the lowest level and allows for the most concurrency; however, it suffers from dirty reads, nonrepeatable reads, and phantom reads.

- READ_COMMITTED – This is the second lowest level and prevents dirty reads, but still suffers from nonrepeatable reads and phantom reads.

- REPEATABLE_READ – This level prevents dirty reads and nonrepeatable reads, with the trade-off of allowing less concurrency, but still suffers from phantom reads.

- SERIALIZABLE – This is the highest level of isolation and prevents all concurrency side effects, with the trade-off of very low concurrency (only one serializable operation can happen at a time).

⚡ To understand these isolation levels, you need to understand the setbacks of concurrent transactions (dirty reads, nonrepeatable reads, and phantom reads). A dirty read is when a single transaction reads data from another concurrent transaction that has not yet committed. A nonrepeatable read is one where another transaction commits new data that is read after already reading different data earlier. A phantom read happens when you get different rows due to another transaction adding or removing rows during the current transaction.

Spring Data R2DBC

R2DBC stands for Reactive Relational Database Connectivity. It is an API for interacting with relational databases like PostgreSQL, H2, and Microsoft SQL asynchronously using reactive types.

Spring Data R2DBC[1] contains a wide range of features:

- Spring configuration support

- A `DatabaseClient` helper interface with a builder that assists in performing common R2DBC operations with integrated object mapping between rows and POJOs

- Exception translation into Spring's Data Access Exceptions

- Feature-rich object mapping integrated with Spring's Conversion Service

- Annotation-based mapping metadata that is extensible to support other metadata formats

- Automatic implementation of `Repository<T,ID>` interfaces, including support for custom query methods

Although the project is relatively young, existing drivers include the following as of writing (with `groupId:artifactId` names):

- Postgres (io.r2dbc:r2dbc-postgresql)

- H2 (io.r2dbc:r2dbc-h2)

- Microsoft SQL Server (io.r2dbc:r2dbc-mssql)

- MySQL (dev.miku:r2dbc-mysql)

Spring Data has an R2DBC integration, and there is a spring-boot-starter-data-r2dbc.

Spring Data R2DBC wraps R2DBC in a familiar fashion. You can create a Repository interface and extend `ReactiveCrudRepository<T,ID>`, and Spring will generate the implementations for you.

---

[1]`https://spring.io/projects/spring-data-r2dbc`

```
public interface PersonRepository
    extends ReactiveCrudRepository<Customer, Long> {
// additional custom query methods go here
}
```

Unlike a normal CrudRepository<T,ID>, the ReactiveCrudRepository <T,ID> methods all return reactive types like Mono and Flux (see Chapter 12 for more about these types). For example, here are some of the methods:

- Mono<Void> delete(T entity) – Deletes the given entity from the database

- Flux<T> findAll() – Returns all instances of the type

- Mono<T> findById(org.reactivestreams. Publisher<ID> id) – Retrieves an entity by its ID, which is supplied by a Publisher

- Mono<S> save(S entity) – Saves a given entity

- Flux<S> saveAll(Iterable<S> entities) – Saves all given entities

- Flux<S> saveAll(org.reactivestreams. Publisher<S> entityStream) – Saves all given entities from a given Publisher

Custom Reactive Queries

You can also specify custom SQL queries using the @Query annotation just like for JPA or JDBC, for example:

```
@Query("SELECT * FROM customer WHERE lastname = :lastname")
Flux<Customer> findByLastname(String lastname);

@Query("SELECT firstname, lastname FROM Customer WHERE
lastname = ?1")
Mono<Customer> findFirstByLastname(String lastname);
```

Kotlin Support

Spring Data R2DBC supports Kotlin 1.3.x in many ways.

It requires kotlin-stdlib (or one of its variants, such as kotlin-stdlib-jdk8) and kotlin-reflect to be present on the classpath (which is provided by default if you bootstrap a Kotlin project via https://start.spring.io).

ℹ️ For more information, see the documentation for Spring Data R2DBC.[2]

---

[2]https://docs.spring.io/spring-data/r2dbc/docs/1.0.0.RELEASE/ reference/html/#reference

CHAPTER 7

Spring MVC

Spring Web MVC is a framework for building web services or web applications and is often shortened to Spring MVC or just MVC. *MVC* stands for Model-View-Controller and is one of the common design patterns in OO (object-oriented) programming.

Core Concepts

Spring MVC is designed with the open-closed principle in mind (open for extension, closed for modification). The DispatchServlet is the core of Spring MVC, and it contains a Servlet WebApplicationContext (containing the controllers, ViewResolver, HandlerMapping, and other resolvers) which delegates to a Root WebApplicationContext (which contains the service and repository beans of the application).

It detects the following types of beans and uses them if found; otherwise, defaults are used: HandlerMapping, HandlerAdapter, HandlerExceptionResolver, ViewResolver, LocaleResolver, ThemeResolver, MultipartResolver, and FlashMapManager.

You can integrate directly with a view technology such as JSP, Velocity, or FreeMarker, or you can return a serialized response like JSON through a ViewResolver or built-in object mapper using DTOs (data transfer objects) or any POJO.

© Adam L. Davis 2020
A. L. Davis, *Spring Quick Reference Guide*, https://doi.org/10.1007/978-1-4842-6144-6_7

DispatcherServlet

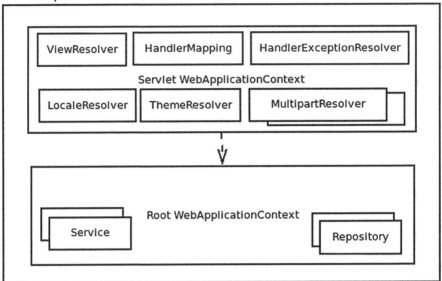

Figure 7-1. *DispatcherServlet*

Getting Started

First, add the dependency to your project.

Then using either Java config or XML (or auto-configuration), enable Web MVC in the project, for example:

Listing 7-1. WebConfig.java

```
import org.springframework.web.servlet.config.annotation.
EnableWebMvc;
import org.springframework.context.annotation.Configuration;
@EnableWebMvc
public class WebConfig {}
```

Also make sure to use @ComponentScan or @Bean or XML bean definitions to define your Spring Beans. In a typical application, you might also have services and repositories, but for this chapter, we will focus only on the Spring Web MVC components.

Controllers

Annotate a class with the @Controller annotation to mark it as a controller. Using @RestController is similar but is used for RESTful web service controllers – it assumes the returned value of every method is converted to a return value, such as JSON (similar to when the method is annotated with @ResponseBody). Using either of these annotations will allow your class to be picked up by component scanning.

You can also annotate the class with @RequestMapping to set a URL prefix that will apply to every method in the class. For example, annotating a controller class with @RequestMapping("/api/v1/") will add the "/api/v1/" prefix to the URL mapping of every method within the controller.

Request Mappings

Annotate a method with @RequestMapping or one of the corresponding HTTP method type annotations, such as @GetMapping. Each method request mapping should match a specific incoming request. If more than one method would match the same HTTP request, Spring will throw an error upon initializing the controller (typically at start-up time).

Each method of the class should be annotated with one of the following to map it to a corresponding URL path:

- @RequestMapping – You need to set the HTTP method and path properties, for example, @RequestMapping(method = RequestMethod. PUT, path = "/courses/{id}").

63

- @GetMapping("/path") – Maps to HTTP GET.

- @PostMapping("/path") – Maps to HTTP POST.

- @DeleteMapping("/path") – Maps to HTTP DELETE.

- @PutMapping("/path") – Maps to HTTP PUT.

- @PatchMapping("/path") – Maps to HTTP PATCH.

You can provide a URL with values embedded within it to define path variables which can be mapped to parameters. For example, in the URL "/images/{filename}/raw", filename corresponds to a path variable:

Listing 7-2. Example get-mapping using path variable and produces

```
@GetMapping(value = "/images/{filename}/raw",
  produces = MediaType.IMAGE_JPEG_VALUE)
public void getImage(@PathVariable String filename,
OutputStream output) {
  // code to send image
}
```

In this example, the given OutputStream parameter can be used to provide the output data (image in this case). You can use produces to set the Content-Type of the response ("image/jpeg" in this case).

You can also annotate a method with @ResponseStatus to change the successful HTTP status to something other than the default (200). For example, the following would change the response status code to 201:

Listing 7-3. Create POST Mapping with custom response status

```
@ResponseStatus(HttpStatus.CREATED)
@PostMapping(value = "/courses",
  consumes = MediaType.APPLICATION_JSON_VALUE)
public void create(@RequestBody final CourseDto course) {
    // code to save
}
```

You can also specify request parameters or header values to make a request mapping even more specific. For example, `@PostMapping(value = "/courses", params = "lang=java", headers = "X-custom-header")` would only match POST requests with a query parameter named "lang" with the value of "java" and a header named X-custom-header present.

Path Regular Expressions

You can also use a regular expression within path variable definitions to limit path matching. For example, the following would only match paths ending with a number:

Listing 7-4. Get Course by Id mapping

```
@GetMapping("/courses/{id:\\d+}")
public CourseDto course(@PathVariable final Long id) {
    // code to get Course
}
```

Mapping Method Parameters

Valid annotations for parameters of a mapped method in a controller are as follows:

- @RequestParam – A query parameter.

- @PathVariable – A part of the path.

- @MatrixVariable – These variables can appear in any part of the path, and the character equals ("=") is used for giving values and the semicolon(";") for delimiting each matrix variable. On the same path, we can also repeat the same variable name or separate different values using the character comma (",").

- @RequestHeader – An HTTP header from the request.

- @CookieValue – A value from a cookie.

- @RequestPart – Annotation that can be used to associate the part of a "multipart/form-data" request with a method argument. Supported method argument types include MultipartFile in conjunction with Spring's MultipartResolver abstraction and javax.servlet.http.Part in conjunction with Servlet 3.0 multipart requests, or otherwise for any other method argument, the content of the part is passed through an HttpMessageConverter taking into consideration the "Content-Type" header of the request part.

- @ModelAttribute – Can be used to get access to an object from the Model. For example, public String handleCustomer(@ModelAttribute("customer") Customer customer) would get the Customer object using the key "customer".

- @SessionAttribute – Attribute of the session.

- @RequestAttribute – Attribute of the request.

⚲ Although Java does not keep parameter names by default in the compiled bytecode, you can achieve this through a setting – Spring Boot does this by default without any intervention needed, allowing you to freely use parameter-name-linked path variables and similar.

Response Body

Annotate a method with @ResponseBody to tell Spring to use the method's return value as the body of the HTTP response.

Alternatively, if you annotate the class with @RestController, this implies the response body is the return value for every method.

Spring will automatically convert the response to the proper value using implementations of HttpMessageConverter. Spring MVC comes with built-in converters.

Other allowed response types are

- HttpEntity

- ResponseEntity<T> – Contains both an entity to be serialized by Spring's conversion logic and HTTP values such as an HTTP status

- HttpHeaders

- String (name of the view to resolve)

- View

- Map or Model

- ModelAndView

- DeferredResult<V>, Callable<V>, ListenableFuture<V>, or CompletableFuture<V> – Asynchronous results

- ResponseBodyEmitter

- SseEmitter

- StreamingResponseBody

- Reactive types like Flux

Views

Spring Web MVC includes support for several different view renderers such as JSP, FreeMarker, Groovy templates, and Velocity. Based on which view technology is chosen, the selected ViewResolver will expose the model, session, and request attributes appropriately.

Spring MVC also includes a JSP tag library to assist in building JSP pages.

Here's an overall diagram summarizing how Spring MVC works, with some details missing such as handling exceptions (we will cover this later):

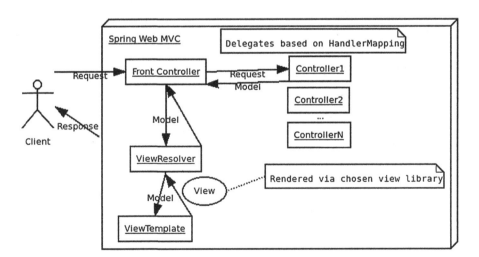

Figure 7-2. *Spring Web MVC request/response*

View Resolvers

Spring supplies several different view resolvers:

ViewResolver	Description
AbstractCaching ViewResolver	Abstract view resolver that caches views. Often views need preparation before they can be used; extending this view resolver provides caching.
XmlViewResolver	Implementation of ViewResolver that accepts a configuration file written in XML with the same DTD as Spring's XML bean factories. The default configuration file is / WEB-INF/views.xml.
ResourceBundle ViewResolver	Implementation of ViewResolver that uses bean definitions in a ResourceBundle, specified by the bundle base name. Typically, you define the bundle in a properties file, located in the classpath. The default file name is views.properties.
UrlBasedViewResolver	Simple implementation of the ViewResolver interface that effects the direct resolution of logical view names to URLs, without an explicit mapping definition. This is appropriate if your logical names match the names of your view resources in a straightforward manner, without the need for arbitrary mappings.

(*continued*)

ViewResolver	Description
`InternalResource` `ViewResolver`	Convenient subclass of `UrlBasedViewResolver` that supports `InternalResourceView` (in effect, Servlets and JSPs) and subclasses such as `JstlView` and `TilesView`. You can specify the view class for all views generated by this resolver by using `setViewClass(..)`.

`VelocityViewResolver/`
`FreeMarkerViewResolver/`
`GroovyMarkupViewResolver`
	Convenient subclasses of `AbstractTemplateViewResolver` that supports `VelocityView` (in effect, Velocity templates), `FreeMarkerView`, or GroovyMarkupView, respectively, and custom subclasses of them.

`ContentNegotiatingView` `Resolver`	Implementation of the `ViewResolver` interface that resolves a view based on the request file name or `Accept` header.

For example, to configure a Spring application to use JSP views, and serving static resources from /images and /styles, you should create a Java configuration class named WebConfig.java like the following:

Listing 7-5. WebConfig.java

```
@Configuration
@EnableWebMvc
@ComponentScan(basePackages = {"com.apress.spring_quick.web"})
public class WebConfig extends WebMvcConfigurerAdapter {
    // Declare our static resources
    @Override
```

```java
public void addResourceHandlers(ResourceHandlerRegistry
registry {
  registry.addResourceHandler("/images/**")
      .addResourceLocations("/images/");
  registry.addResourceHandler("/styles/**")
      .addResourceLocations("/styles/");
}
@Override
public void configureDefaultServletHandling(
            DefaultServletHandlerConfigurer configurer) {
    configurer.enable();
}
// Serves up /WEB-INF/home.jsp for both "/" and "/home"
   paths:
@Override
public void addViewControllers(ViewControllerRegistry
registry) {
    registry.addViewController("/").setViewName("home");
    registry.addViewController("/home").setViewName
    ("home");
}
@Bean
InternalResourceViewResolver getViewResolver() {
    InternalResourceViewResolver resolver =
        new InternalResourceViewResolver();
    resolver.setPrefix("/WEB-INF/");
    resolver.setSuffix(".jsp" );
    resolver.setRequestContextAttribute("requestContext");
    return resolver;
}
```

This sets up a web application with the InternalResourceViewResolver that looks for files under the "/WEB-INF" directory with ".jsp" file extensions.

Error Handling

You can declare a custom error handler method using the @ExceptionHandler annotation. Spring calls this method when a request handler method throws any of the specified exceptions.

The caught exception can be passed to the method as an argument. For example, see the following method:

Listing 7-6. Custom handleArgException method

```
@ExceptionHandler(IllegalArgumentException.class)
@ResponseStatus(HttpStatus.BAD_REQUEST)
public void handleArgException(IllegalArgumentException
exception) {
    // Log the exception
}
```

Note how we use @ResponseStatus to change the HTTP status code to 400 (Bad Request) returned in this case. This however does not change the resulting view rendered of the Exception. You can override the content directly by annotating the method with @ResponseBody and returning a value, for example:

Listing 7-7. Custom handleArgException method which returns a DTO

```
@ExceptionHandler(IllegalArgumentException.class)
@ResponseStatus(HttpStatus.BAD_REQUEST)
public ExceptionDto handleArgException(IllegalArgument
Exception ex) {
    return new ExceptionDto(ex);
}
```

To handle Exceptions throughout all of the controllers in your application, you can use a class annotated with @ControllerAdvice and put all of your methods marked with @ExceptionHandler there.

Web Scopes

Additional scopes exist in a web application:

- "application" – The application scope creates the bean instance for the life cycle of a ServletContext, which could span multiple servlet-based applications.

- "request" – The *request* scope creates a bean instance for a single HTTP request.

- "session" – The *session* scope creates a bean for an HTTP Session.

Testing

Spring typically provides test support for all of its projects. Since everything is a POJO, it is straightforward to write unit tests. For Spring MVC, Spring Boot provides the @WebMvcTest annotation to put on a test class and MvcMock type that helps test controllers without too much performance overhead.

For example, to get started with a Spring Boot with Spring MVC Gradle–based build, start with the following Gradle build file:

Listing 7-8. build.gradle

```
plugins {
  id 'org.springframework.boot' version '2.2.6.RELEASE'
  id 'io.spring.dependency-management' version '1.0.9.RELEASE'
  id 'java'
}
group = 'com.apress.spring-quick'
version = '0.0.1-SNAPSHOT'
sourceCompatibility = '11'

repositories {
  mavenLocal()
  mavenCentral()
}
dependencies {
  implementation 'org.springframework.boot:spring-boot-
  starter-web'
  testImplementation('org.springframework.boot:spring-
  boot-starter-test') {
    exclude group: 'org.junit.vintage', module: 'junit-
    vintage-engine'
  }
}
test {
  useJUnitPlatform()
}
```

Then create a JUnit 5–based test class named ControllerTest like the following within the same package as your application's main configuration file (or in a subpackage):

Listing 7-9. ControllerTest.java

```
import com.apress.spring_quick.jpa.simple.Course;
import com.apress.spring_quick.jpa.simple.
SimpleCourseRepository;
import org.junit.jupiter.api.Test;
import org.junit.jupiter.api.extension.ExtendWith;
import org.springframework.beans.factory.annotation.Autowired;
import org.springframework.boot.test.autoconfigure.web.servlet.
WebMvcTest;
import org.springframework.boot.test.mock.mockito.MockBean;
import org.springframework.test.context.junit.jupiter.
SpringExtension;
import org.springframework.test.web.servlet.MockMvc;
import java.util.List;
import static org.hamcrest.Matchers.containsString;
import static org.mockito.Mockito.when;
import static org.springframework.test.web.servlet.request.
MockMvcRequestBuilders.get;
import static org.springframework.test.web.servlet.result.
MockMvcResultHandlers.print;
import static org.springframework.test.web.servlet.result.
MockMvcResultMatchers.content;
import static org.springframework.test.web.servlet.result.
MockMvcResultMatchers.status;
```

```
@ExtendWith(SpringExtension.class) //(1)
@WebMvcTest                        //(2)
public class ControllerTest {

    @Autowired
    private MockMvc mockMvc;
    @MockBean
    private SimpleCourseRepository courseRepository;

    @Test
    public void coursesShouldReturnAllCourses() throws
    Exception {
        Course course = new Course();
        course.setName("Java Professional");
        course.setSubtitle("Java 11");
        course.setDescription("");
        when(courseRepository.findAll()).thenReturn(List.
        of(course));
        mockMvc.perform(get("/api/v1/courses"))            //(3)
                .andDo(print()).andExpect(status().isOk())
                .andExpect(content().string(
        containsString("[{\"id\":null,\"title\":\"Java
        Professional\"" +
          ",\"subtitle\":\"Java 11\",\"description\":
          \"\"}]")));
    }
}
```

1. Using @ExtendWith with SpringExtension enables
    Spring's testing helper to scan for things like the
    @MockBean annotation which creates a bean which
    is a (mockito) mock instance.

2. Using @WebMvcTest causes Spring to auto-
    configure only the MVC layer of the application,
    including controllers.

3. Calling perform on the instance of MockMvc
    invokes the HandlerMapping logic and has a fluent
    interface for validating the response. In this case,
    we use ".andDo(print())" to print it out and then
    expect the HTTP status to be OK (200) and use
    "content().string(containsString(String))" to
    validate that the response string has the expected
    result.

Without Spring Boot auto-configuration, you can also create a
MockMvc instance using the MockMvcBuilders.*webAppContextSetup(Web*
ApplicationContext) method, for example:

```
// imports:
import static org.springframework.test.web.servlet.setup.
MockMvcBuilders.*;
// ...code:
WebApplicationContext wac = /** Create the application context
*/;
MockMvc mockMvc = webAppContextSetup(wac).build();
```

CHAPTER 8

Spring Mobile

Spring Mobile is an extension to Spring MVC that aims to simplify the development of mobile web applications. It includes a module for detecting on the server the type of device, mobile, tablet, or desktop making a request.

Getting Started

Include the project in your dependencies, for example, in a Maven pom:

```
<dependency>
    <groupId>org.springframework.mobile</groupId>
    <artifactId>spring-mobile-device</artifactId>
    <version>${org.springframework.mobile-version}</version>
</dependency>
```

In a Gradle build file, add the following under dependencies:

```
implementation
  "org.springframework.mobile:spring-mobile-
  device:$mobileVersion"
```

Then set the version[1] in your `gradle.properties` file:

```
mobileVersion=1.1.5.RELEASE
```

Next, add either the `DeviceResolverHandlerInterceptor` or `DeviceResolverRequestFilter` to your web application. The first is more tightly coupled to the Spring framework, while the second is an implementation of a servlet filter, so less coupled to Spring.

DeviceResolverHandlerInterceptor

Spring Mobile ships with a `HandlerInterceptor` that, on `preHandle`, delegates to a `DeviceResolver`. The resolved `Device` is set as a request attribute named "`currentDevice`", making it available to handlers throughout the request processing.

To enable, add the `DeviceResolverHandlerInterceptor` to the list of interceptors defined in your `DispatcherServlet` configuration XML:

```xml
<interceptors>
  <bean class="org.springframework.mobile.device.
  DeviceResolverHandlerInterceptor" />
</interceptors>
```

Alternatively, you can add the `DeviceResolverHandlerInterceptor` using Spring's *Java-based configuration*:

```java
@Configuration
@EnableWebMvc
@ComponentScan
```

---

[1]The latest milestone release is 2.0.0.M3 at the time of writing, so 2.0.0 may be released by the time you read this.

```
public class WebConfig implements WebMvcConfigurer {
//...
  @Bean
  public DeviceResolverHandlerInterceptor drhInterceptor() {
      return new DeviceResolverHandlerInterceptor();
  }
  @Override
  public void addInterceptors(InterceptorRegistry registry) {
      registry.addInterceptor(drhInterceptor());
  }
}
```

DeviceResolverRequestFilter

As an alternative to the DeviceResolverHandlerInterceptor, Spring
Mobile also ships with a servlet filter that delegates to a DeviceResolver.
As with the HandlerInterceptor, the resolved Device is set under a
request attribute named "currentDevice".

To enable, add the DeviceResolverRequestFilter to your web.xml
as follows:

```
<filter>
  <filter-name>deviceResolverRequestFilter</filter-name>
  <filter-class>
org.springframework.mobile.device.DeviceResolverRequestFilter
  </filter-class>
</filter>
```

Accessing the Device

To look up the current Device in your code, you can do so in several ways. If you already have a reference to a ServletRequest or Spring WebRequest, simply use DeviceUtils:

```
//imports
import org.springframework.mobile.device.DeviceUtils;
// code...
Device currentDevice = DeviceUtils.getCurrentDevice(servlet
Request);
```

This would get the current device or null if no device has been resolved for the request. There's also a getRequiredCurrentDevice(HttpServlet Request request) method that throws a runtime exception if the current device has not been resolved.

The Device interface has the following methods available:

Return Type	Method
DevicePlatform	getDevicePlatform() – Returns an enum which can be IOS, ANDROID, or UNKNOWN.
Boolean	isMobile() – True if this device is a mobile device such as an Apple iPhone or a Nexus One Android.
Boolean	isNormal() – True if this device is not a mobile or tablet device.
Boolean	isTablet() – True if this device is a tablet device such as an Apple iPad or a Motorola Xoom.

DeviceWebArgumentResolver

If you'd like to pass the current Device automatically as an argument to one or more of your controller methods, configure a DeviceWebArgumentResolver using XML:

```
<annotation-driven>
  <argument-resolvers>
    <bean class="org.springframework.mobile.device.DeviceWeb
    ArgumentResolver" />
  </argument-resolvers>
</annotation-driven>
```

You can alternatively configure a DeviceHandlerMethodArgument Resolver using a Java-based configuration like the following:

```
@Bean
public DeviceHandlerMethodArgumentResolver deviceHMAR() {
    return new DeviceHandlerMethodArgumentResolver();
}
@Override
public void addArgumentResolvers(
List<HandlerMethodArgumentResolver> argumentResolvers) {
  argumentResolvers.add(deviceHMAR());
}
```

LiteDeviceResolver

Spring allows for different implementations of DeviceResolver, but by default provides an implementation which only detects the presence of a mobile or tablet device named LiteDeviceResolver.

83

You can also customize the LiteDeviceResolver by adding additional keywords that, if contained in a request's User-Agent, will resolve as a "normal" device, for example, using Java configuration:

```
@Bean
public LiteDeviceResolver liteDeviceResolver() {
    List<String> keywords = new ArrayList<String>();
    keywords.add("vivaldi");
    keywords.add("yandex");
    return new LiteDeviceResolver(keywords);
}
@Bean
public DeviceResolverHandlerInterceptor
deviceResolverHandlerInt() {
    return new DeviceResolverHandlerInterceptor(liteDevice
    Resolver());
}
@Override
public void addInterceptors(InterceptorRegistry registry) {
    registry.addInterceptor(deviceResolverHandlerInt());
}
```

Site Preference Management

Spring Mobile provides a single SitePreferenceHandler implementation named StandardSitePreferenceHandler, which should be suitable for most needs. It supports a query parameter–based site preference indication (site_preference) and pluggable SitePreference storage and may be enabled in a Spring MVC application using the SitePreferenceHandlerInterceptor. In addition, if a SitePreference has not been explicitly indicated by the user, a default will be derived based on the user's Device detected.

So along with the previous interceptors, add the following:

```
@Bean
public SitePreferenceHandlerInterceptor
    sitePreferenceHandlerInterceptor() {
    return new SitePreferenceHandlerInterceptor();
}
```

Then update the addInterceptors method to the following:

```
@Override
public void addInterceptors(InterceptorRegistry registry) {
    registry.addInterceptor(drhInterceptor());
    registry.addInterceptor(sitePreferenceHandler
    Interceptor());
}
```

Similarly to the Device resolution, you can gain access to the current SitePreference using either the SitePreferenceUtils or SitePreferenceHandlerMethodArgumentResolver. However, it might make more sense to redirect mobile users to a different site. In this case, you may use the SiteSwitcherHandlerInterceptor to redirect mobile users to a dedicated mobile site.

The mDot, dotMobi, urlPath, and standard factory methods of SitePreferenceHandlerInterceptor configure the cookie-based SitePreference storage. The cookie value will be shared across the mobile and normal site domains. Internally, the interceptor delegates to a SitePreferenceHandler, so there is no need to register a SitePreferenceHandlerInterceptor when using the switcher. For example, the following Interceptor would redirect mobile users to mobile. app.com, tablets to tablet.app.com, and otherwise just app.com:

```
@Bean
public SiteSwitcherHandlerInterceptor
siteSwitcherHandlerInterceptor() {
    return SiteSwitcherHandlerInterceptor.standard("app.com",
        "mobile.app.com", "tablet.app.com", ".app.com");
}
// standard(normalName, mobileServerName, tabletServerName,
   cookieDomain)
```

A simpler method that does not require additional DNS entries is the urlPath factory:

```
@Bean
public SiteSwitcherHandlerInterceptor
siteSwitcherHandlerInterceptor() {
    return SiteSwitcherHandlerInterceptor.urlPath("/mobile");
}
```

This Interceptor would redirect mobile users to <your app>/mobile/ paths. For example, if the normal URL is "myapp.com/courses", then the mobile site will be "myapp.com/mobile/courses".

Spring Mobile Example

This example will build on the Spring Web MVC and Spring Data content from the previous chapters, as well as making use of Spring Boot. For more information on either topic, please see the related chapter. This example project is available online.[2]

---

[2]https://github.com/adamldavis/spring-quick-ref

To get started, create a new directory named "spring-mobile" and create a Gradle "build.gradle" file like the following:

Listing 8-1. build.gradle

```
plugins {
    id 'org.springframework.boot' version '2.3.1.RELEASE'
    id 'io.spring.dependency-management' version
    '1.0.9.RELEASE'
    id "java"
}
group = 'com.apress.spring-quick'
version = '0.0.1-SNAPSHOT'
sourceCompatibility = '11'

ext {
    mobileVersion = '1.1.5.RELEASE'
}
repositories {
    mavenLocal()
    mavenCentral()
}
dependencies {
    implementation "org.springframework.boot:spring-boot-
    starter-actuator"
    implementation "org.springframework.boot:spring-boot-
    starter-web"
    implementation "org.springframework.boot:spring-boot-
    starter-groovy-templates"
    implementation "org.springframework.mobile:spring-mobile-
    device:$mobileVersion"
```

```
    implementation "com.apress.spring-quick:spring-data-
    jpa:0.0.1"

    implementation "com.h2database:h2:1.4.192" // database
}
```

This uses the Spring Boot Gradle plugin and dependency management to simplify setting up the project. Note that we include the "spring-data-jpa" project from Chapter 6 as a dependency. This makes the repositories available for potential inclusion as Spring beans at runtime (depending on the configuration).

Next, create a main class, like the following:

Listing 8-2. SpringMobileWebApp.java

```
@SpringBootApplication
@Import({WebConfig.class, ServiceConfig.class})
public class SpringMobileWebApp {
    public static void main(String[] args) throws IOException {
        SpringApplication.run(SpringMobileWebApp.class, args);
    }
}
```

Next, set up the ServiceConfig, which includes specific packages from the "spring-data-jpa" project from Chapter 6:

```
@Configuration
@EnableJpaRepositories(basePackages =
        {"com.apress.spring_quick.jpa.simple", "com.apress.
        spring_quick.jpa.compositions"},
        enableDefaultTransactions = true)
@ComponentScan(basePackages = {"com.apress.spring_quick.jpa.
simple", "com.apress.spring_quick.jpa.compositions"})
public class ServiceConfig {
}
```

Next, we specify the WebConfig class, which defines Interceptors as described previously in this chapter, as well as GroovyMarkupConfigurer and GroovyMarkupViewResolver:

Listing 8-3. WebConfig.java

```
import org.springframework.context.annotation.*;
import org.springframework.web.servlet.config.annotation.*;
import org.springframework.mobile.device.*;
import org.springframework.mobile.device.site.*;
import org.springframework.mobile.device.switcher.*;
import org.springframework.web.method.support.*;
@Configuration
@EnableWebMvc
@ComponentScan
public class WebConfig implements WebMvcConfigurer {

    @Bean
    public SitePreferenceHandlerMethodArgumentResolver
    sitePrefMAR() {
        return new SitePreferenceHandlerMethod
        ArgumentResolver();
    }
    @Bean
    public DeviceHandlerMethodArgumentResolver deviceHMAR() {
        return new DeviceHandlerMethodArgumentResolver();
    }

    @Override
    public void addArgumentResolvers(List<HandlerMethodArgument
    Resolver> argumentResolvers) {
        argumentResolvers.add(deviceHMAR());
        argumentResolvers.add(sitePrefMAR());
    }
```

```
@Bean
public DeviceResolverHandlerInterceptor drhInterceptor() {
    return new DeviceResolverHandlerInterceptor();
}

@Bean
public SitePreferenceHandlerInterceptor
sitePreferenceHandlerInterceptor() {
    return new SitePreferenceHandlerInterceptor();
}

@Bean
public SiteSwitcherHandlerInterceptor
siteSwitcherHandlerInterceptor(){
    return SiteSwitcherHandlerInterceptor.urlPath("/mobile");
}

@Override
public void addInterceptors(InterceptorRegistry registry) {
    registry.addInterceptor(drhInterceptor());
    registry.addInterceptor(sitePreferenceHandler
    Interceptor());
    registry.addInterceptor(siteSwitcherHandlerInterceptor());
}

@Bean
public GroovyMarkupConfigurer groovyMarkupConfigurer() {
    GroovyMarkupConfigurer configurer = new
    GroovyMarkupConfigurer();
    configurer.setResourceLoaderPath("classpath:/
    templates/");
    return configurer;
}
```

```
@Bean
public GroovyMarkupViewResolver groovyMarkupViewResolver() {
    GroovyMarkupViewResolver resolver = new GroovyMarkup
    ViewResolver();
    resolver.setSuffix(".groovy");
    resolver.setRequestContextAttribute("requestContext");
    return resolver;
}
}
```

Note that we've defined a SiteSwitcherHandlerInterceptor using the "/mobile" path. The Groovy-related configuration tells Spring to look under /templates/ in the classpath for files ending in ".groovy".

Finally, we need to define the controllers for our MVC application. To enable a completely different logic for mobile sites, we can define a separate controller for mobile vs. normal requests. Alternatively, we could inject SitePreference as a method parameter to each controller method and use that instead since we set up a SitePreferenceHandlerMethodArgumentResolver.

In this case, we create a CourseController and MobileCourseController, which should look like the following:

Listing 8-4. CourseController.java

```
@Controller
@RequestMapping
public class CourseController {
    @GetMapping("/")
    public String home() {
        return "home";
    }
    // additional methods...
```

Listing 8-5. MobileCourseController.java

```
@Controller
@RequestMapping("/mobile")
public class MobileCourseController {
    @GetMapping("/")
    public String home() {
        return "mobile/home";
    }
    // additional methods...
```

Note that since the MobileCourseController is annotated with
@RequestMapping("/mobile"), it will match all paths starting with
"/mobile", hence all users with the SitePreference of Mobile. Similarly,
we could do the same for Tablet.

The Groovy markup templates should be placed under the src/main/
resources/templates directory. The "home.groovy" template should look
something like the following:

```
yieldUnescaped '<!DOCTYPE html>'
html(lang:'en') {
    head {
        meta('http-equiv':'"Content-Type" content: "text/html;
        charset: utf-8"')
        title('Courses Demo')
        link(rel: 'stylesheet', href: '/styles/main.css',
        type: 'text/css')
    }
    body {
        h3('Normal Home page')
        div(class: 'site_pref') {
            a(href: '/?site_preference=mobile', 'Mobile')
```

```
            yieldUnescaped '|'
            a(href: '/?site_preference=normal', 'Desktop')
        }
        div(class: 'content') {
            div {
                a(href: '/courses', 'Courses')
            }
        }
    }
}
```

Using the URL *?site_preference=mobile* (or clicking the "Mobile" link on the web page which has the same URL path) triggers the SiteSwitcherHandlerInterceptor to change the SitePreference. In this case, the user would be redirected to the "mobile/home" view which is rendered by the file src/main/resources/templates/mobile/home.groovy.

Figure 8-1. *Mobile/normal home page*

✏ EXERCISE: ADD TABLETS

Starting with the code from this chapter (which is available online[3]), add support for tablets.

---

[3]https://github.com/adamldavis/spring-quick-ref

CHAPTER 9

Spring Security

Spring Security is a highly customizable authentication and access control framework. It is the standard for securing Spring-based applications. It includes support for a variety of security standards such as LDAP and OAuth2.

In addition, it integrates well with the other Spring modules and projects and can make use of annotation-based proxies. In addition, it works well with SpEL (Spring Expression Language) which we will cover in this chapter.

Features

Spring Security is easily extended and has many built-in features:

- Comprehensive and extensible support for both Authentication and Authorization

- Protection against attacks like session fixation, clickjacking, cross-site request forgery, and so on

- Servlet API integration

- Optional integration with Spring Web MVC

- Support for OAuth and OAuth2

- Support for SAML

© Adam L. Davis 2020
A. L. Davis, *Spring Quick Reference Guide*, https://doi.org/10.1007/978-1-4842-6144-6_9

Overview

Spring Security at its core is divided into two things: *authentication*, which decides the identity of the user (principal), and *access control*, which decides what users gain access to what resources.

Spring Security authentication is based around an AuthenticationManager interface which has one method, Authentication authenticate(Authentication). It is implemented by a ProviderManager which has one or more AuthenticationProviders. The AuthenticationProvider interface has two methods, Authentication authenticate(Authentication) and boolean supports(Class) which returns true if this AuthenticationProvider supports the indicated Authentication object.

Spring Security access control (also known as authorization) is based around an AccessDecisionManager which has one or more AccessDecisionVoters. The primary implementation of AccessDecisionVoter<S> is the RoleVoter which makes access decisions based on roles.

Configuration

Spring Security can be configured through the typical means, XML or Java configuration.

Listing 9-1. SecurityConfig.java

```
import org.springframework.http.HttpMethod;
import org.springframework.security.config.annotation.
authentication.builders.*;
import org.springframework.security.config.annotation.web.
builders.HttpSecurity;
```

```
import org.springframework.security.config.annotation.web.
configuration.*;
import org.springframework.security.core.userdetails.User;
import org.springframework.stereotype.Component;

@Component
public class SecurityConfig extends
WebSecurityConfigurerAdapter {

    // from WebSecurityConfigurerAdapter
    @Override
    protected void configure(AuthenticationManagerBuilder auth)
    throws Exception {
        // here you could configure a JDBC database
        // auth.jdbcAuthentication().usersByUsernameQuery(...)
        auth.inMemoryAuthentication()
                .withUser(User.builder().withDefault
                PasswordEncoder() //(1)
                        .username("admin").password("123")
                        .roles("USER", "ADMIN")
                        .build());
    }

    // from WebSecurityConfigurerAdapter
    @Override
    protected void configure(HttpSecurity http) throws
    Exception {    //(2)
        http.httpBasic().and()
                .authorizeRequests()
                .antMatchers("/courses").hasRole("USER")  //(3)
                .antMatchers(HttpMethod.GET, "/actuator/**").
                permitAll()
                .anyRequest().authenticated()
```

```
                    .and()
                    .formLogin()
                    .loginPage("/login")
                    .permitAll()
                    .and()
                    .logout()
                    .permitAll()
                    .and().csrf().disable();
        }
}
```

1. We declare that the AuthenticationManager should
    use an in-memory user database and add a default
    "admin" user. In production, you should probably
    store users in a database or use some other method.
    For demo purposes, we create a user using the User
    builder method withDefaultPasswordEncoder().
    This should also not be done in production. The
    user is also given the USER and ADMIN roles.

2. The configure(HttpSecurity http) provides a fluent
    interface for use to configure access control using
    URL matchers, login and logout pages, and other
    web security settings. The first method called,
    httpBasic(), enabled HTTP Basic Authentication
    which is header based. The subsequent method,
    and().authorizeRequests(), sets up the authorization
    (access control) settings.

3. The code `antMatchers("/courses")`.
    `hasRole("USER")` creates a filter for the "/courses"
    path only and specifies that the user must have the
    USER role to gain access.

Instead of antMatchers, you can use mvcMatchers, with the main difference being that the latter matches URLs exactly how the MVC @RequestMapping would, which allows for more flexibility such as different extensions (e.g., .json or .xml).

The first matched URL decides the access, so you should order the URL matchers from most specific to least specific.

Password Security

Passwords in Spring Security are encrypted via an implementation of the PasswordEncoder interface, which Spring provides several implementations (there is no decoder since password encoding should be a one-way algorithm).

NoOpPasswordEncoder	A password encoder that does nothing. Useful for testing where working with plaintext passwords may be preferred.
BCryptPasswordEncoder	An implementation of PasswordEncoder that uses the BCrypt strong hashing function.
Pbkdf2PasswordEncoder	A PasswordEncoder implementation that uses PBKDF2 with a configurable number of iterations and a random 8-byte random salt value.
SCryptPasswordEncoder	An implementation of PasswordEncoder that uses the SCrypt hashing function.
StandardPasswordEncoder	A standard PasswordEncoder implementation that uses SHA-256 hashing with 1024 iterations and a random 8-byte random salt value.
DelegatingPasswordEncoder	A password encoder that delegates to another PasswordEncoder based upon a prefixed identifier. This allows for easier encryption upgrading.

If you are developing a new system, the Spring team suggests you use BCryptPasswordEncoder for better security and interoperability with other languages.

You can create a DelegatingPasswordEncoder using PasswordEncoderFactories[1] or through the constructor.

⚠️ To ensure proper security, you should tune your password encoding to take about one second of processing on your system. This helps make passwords harder to crack through brute force. For example, the constructor for BCryptPasswordEncoder can take a strength parameter which specifies the log rounds to use (between 4 and 31), and you should test to find out which number makes encoding take about one second on a decent processor.

Accessing the Authentication

The SecurityContext interface can be used to access the currently logged in user via the getAuthentication() method which obtains the currently authenticated principal or an authentication request token. The SecurityContext can be accessed from the SecurityContextHolder. getContext() static method. By default, the SecurityContextHolder uses ThreadLocal to store the current SecurityContext, which stores a value per Thread.

Spring will inject the value of any parameter of type Principal or Authentication on a controller method.

---

[1]See https://bit.ly/2WAAWEf for more information.

Annotation Security

You can enable access control via annotations. Several different annotations can be used, depending on your project's configuration including @RolesAllowed from the javax.annotation.security package, @Secured, @PreAuthorize, and @PostAuthorize.

First of all, to use Spring Method Security, we need to add the *spring-security-config* dependency, for example, using Maven:

```
<dependency>
    <groupId>org.springframework.security</groupId>
    <artifactId>spring-security-config</artifactId>
    <version>5.3.2.RELEASE</version>
</dependency>
```

If we want to use Spring Boot, we can use the *spring-boot-starter-security* dependency which includes *spring-security-config (see Chapter 15 for more information)*.

Enabling via XML:

Listing 9-2. security.xml

```
<beans ...
    http://www.springframework.org/schema/security
    http://www.springframework.org/schema/security/
    spring-security.xsd">
    <security:global-method-security
        secured-annotations="enabled"
        pre-post-annotations="enabled" />
```

Using Java configuration:

Listing 9-3. MethodSecurityConfig.java

```
@Configuration
@EnableGlobalMethodSecurity(
  prePostEnabled = true, // (1)
  securedEnabled = true, // (2)
  jsr250Enabled = true) //  (3)
public class MethodSecurityConfig
  extends GlobalMethodSecurityConfiguration {
}
```

1. The prePostEnabled property determines if @PreAuthorize and @PostAuthorize should be enabled.

2. The securedEnabled property determines if the @Secured annotation should be enabled.

3. The jsr250Enabled property allows us to use the @RolesAllowed,[2] @PermitAll, and @DenyAll annotations.

Using @Secured

Using the global method security, you can add @Secured on any method on any Spring bean, and it will be intercepted by Spring Security to perform proper authorization.

---

[2]The @RolesAllowed annotation is the JSR-250's equivalent annotation of the @Secured annotation.

For example:

```
@Secured("ROLE_USER")
// method1
@Secured({"ROLE_ADMIN", "ROLE_USER"}) //either ADMIN or USER
// method2
```

@Secured can take an array of strings for multiple roles, in which case if any role is matched, it is allowed. It does not support SpEL (Spring Expression Language), so for more complex access logic, you need to use different annotations.

Using PreAuthorize

Using @PreAuthorize and @PostAuthorize enables much more complex logic (including SpEL which is described subsequently) in determining which users have access.

For example, you might use @PreAuthorize as follows:

```
//imports
import org.springframework.security.access.prepost.
PreAuthorize;
// code...
@PreAuthorize("hasRole('ADMIN') && hasRole('USER')")
public void deleteById(Long id) {
```

In this case, the current authentication must have both ADMIN and USER roles to access the deleteById method.

Expressions provided to @PreAuthorize and @PostAuthorize annotations can also reference additional variables, returnObject for @PostAuthorize, and method parameters (using the *#name* syntax) in @PreAuthorize.

Assume the principal is a User with a username property and a Course has an owner property that might match a User's username for the following examples:

```
@PostAuthorize("returnObject.owner == authentication.principal.
username")
public Course getCourse(Long id) {
  //method definition
}

@PreAuthorize("#course.owner == authentication.principal.
username")
public void removeCourse(Course course) {
  //method definition
}
```

In the first example, the expression will validate that the returned Course object's owner is equal to the Spring Security's authentication's principal's username (the username of the current logged in User). If not the case, the user would get an authentication exception.

The second example validates that the given course's owner is equal to Spring Security's authentication's principal's username before even invoking the method (removeCourse in this case).

Global Method Security
SpEL

SpEL (Spring Expression Language) is a text-based expression language that is interpreted by Spring and is typically used to simplify value injection. It can be used directly within @PreAuthorize and @PostAuthorize values with additional functions available from Spring Security.

SPRING EXPRESSION LANGUAGE

SpEL can be used within any @Value annotation value using the #{*expression*}
syntax. SpEL supports the standard operations (+ - / % < > <= >= ==
!= && || !) as well as their English word equivalents (plus, minus, div, mod,
lt, gt, le, ge, eq, ne, and, or, not). It also supports the Elvis operator (?:) and
null-safe dereference (?.). It also supports "matches" for regular expression
matching.

String values may be specified using single quotes (').

SpEL supports referencing Java types using the T(*Type*) syntax.

SpEL supports defining maps using the {key:value} syntax, for example,
{'key': 1, 'key2': 2}.

It also supports accessing list values by index using the list[n] syntax; for
example, list[0] would access the first element.

Within a Spring Security context, the hasRole function is available so that
hasRole('ADMIN') will return true only if the current user has the ADMIN role.

CHAPTER 10

Spring Web Services

Spring Web Services (Spring WS) is focused on building contract-first SOAP web services, with flexible XML mappings, loose coupling between contract and implementation, and easy integration with Spring. It has an architecture similar to that of Spring MVC.

Features

Spring WS has the following features:

- Powerful mappings – You can distribute incoming XML request to any object, depending on the message payload, SOAP Action header, or an XPath expression.

- XML API support – Incoming XML messages can be handled in standard JAXP APIs such as DOM, SAX, and StAX, but also JDOM, dom4j, XOM, or even marshalling technologies.

- Flexible XML marshalling – The Object/XML Mapping module in the Spring Web Services distribution supports JAXB 1 and 2, Castor, XMLBeans, JiBX, and XStream.

© Adam L. Davis 2020
A. L. Davis, *Spring Quick Reference Guide*, https://doi.org/10.1007/978-1-4842-6144-6_10

- Supports WS-Security – WS-Security allows you to sign SOAP messages, encrypt and decrypt them, or authenticate against them.

- Integrates with Spring Security – The WS-Security implementation of Spring Web Services provides integration with Spring Security.

Getting Started

To get started, add the following dependencies to your Maven pom file:

```
<dependencies>
    <dependency>
        <groupId>org.springframework.ws</groupId>
        <artifactId>spring-ws-core</artifactId>
        <version>3.0.9.RELEASE</version>
    </dependency>
    <dependency>
        <groupId>jdom</groupId>
        <artifactId>jdom</artifactId>
        <version>2.0.2</version>
    </dependency>
    <dependency>
        <groupId>jaxen</groupId>
        <artifactId>jaxen</artifactId>
        <version>1.2.0</version>
    </dependency>
</dependencies>
```

Or if using Gradle, add the following:

```
implementation 'org.springframework.ws:spring-ws-core:3.0.9.
RELEASE'
implementation 'org.jdom:jdom:2.0.2'
implementation 'jaxen:jaxen:1.2.0'
```

Use the @EnableWs annotation on a Java configuration class to enable the spring-ws to register the default EndpointMappings, EndpointAdapter, and EndpointExceptionResolver.

You will need to create a web.xml file like the following:

Listing 10-1. WEB-INF/web.xml

```
<web-app xmlns="http://java.sun.com/xml/ns/j2ee"
         xmlns:xsi="http://www.w3.org/2001/XMLSchema-instance"
         xsi:schemaLocation="http://java.sun.com/xml/ns/j2ee
             http://java.sun.com/xml/ns/j2ee/web-app_2_4.xsd"
         version="2.4">
    <display-name>MyCompany Web Service</display-name>

    <servlet>
        <servlet-name>no-boot-spring-ws</servlet-name>
        <servlet-class>org.springframework.ws.transport.http.
        MessageDispatcherServlet
        </servlet-class>
    </servlet>

    <servlet-mapping>
        <servlet-name>spring-ws</servlet-name>
        <url-pattern>/*</url-pattern>
    </servlet-mapping>

</web-app>
```

Based on the name of the servlet, Spring will look for a corresponding Spring XML configuration file named `<servlet_name>-servlet.xml`. In this case, it will look for a `WEB-INF/no-boot-spring-ws-servlet.xml` file.

Spring Boot Config

To include Spring-WS in a Spring Boot Gradle project, add the following dependencies:

```
implementation 'org.springframework.boot:spring-boot-starter-web-services'
implementation 'org.jdom:jdom:2.0.2'
implementation 'jaxen:jaxen:1.2.0'
```

The Spring Boot WS starter (spring-boot-starter-web-services) will automatically do the following:

- Configure a `MessageDispatcherServlet` in the servlet container

- Scan all **.wsdl** and **.xsd** documents for WSDL and schema-defined beans

Contract First

Writing the contract first enables more features of the actual schema (such as limiting the allowed values of String values), allows for easier upgrading in the future, and allows for better interoperability with non-Java systems.

There are four different ways of defining such a contract for XML:

- DTDs

- XML Schema (XSD)

- RELAX NG[1]

- Schematron[2]

For this book, we will use the XML Schema for the Course domain. For example (assuming you want to use the namespace, `"http://mycompany.com/schemas"`), create a file named "my.xsd" and put it in the "src/main/resources" directory of your project with these contents:

```
<xs:schema xmlns:xs="http://www.w3.org/2001/XMLSchema"
           elementFormDefault="qualified"
           targetNamespace="http://mycompany.com/schemas"
           xmlns:my="http://mycompany.com/schemas">
    <xs:element name="Course">
        <xs:complexType>
            <xs:sequence>
                <xs:element ref="my:Number"/>
                <xs:element ref="my:Title"/>
                <xs:element ref="my:Subtitle"/>
                <xs:element ref="my:Description"/>
            </xs:sequence>
        </xs:complexType>
    </xs:element>
    <xs:element name="Number" type="xs:integer"/>
    <xs:element name="Title" type="xs:string"/>
    <xs:element name="Subtitle" type="xs:string"/>
    <xs:element name="Description" type="xs:string"/>
</xs:schema>
```

In Spring-WS, writing the WSDL by hand is not required. We will show how to generate the WSDL in a later section.

---

[1]`https://relaxng.org/`
[2]`http://schematron.com/`

Writing the Endpoint

In Spring-WS, you will implement *Endpoints* to handle incoming XML messages. An endpoint is typically created by annotating a class with the @Endpoint annotation with one or more methods that handle incoming requests. The method signatures can be quite flexible: you can include just about any sort of parameter type related to the incoming XML message, as will be explained later.

Start by creating a class annotated with @Endpoint that will either be component scanned (@Endpoint marks it as a special @Component) or directly use Java configuration to configure it as a Spring Bean. Then add a method or methods that handle different elements of an XML request, for example:

```
import org.jdom2.*;
import org.jdom2.filter.Filters;
import org.jdom2.xpath.XPathExpression;
import org.jdom2.xpath.XPathFactory;
import org.springframework.beans.factory.annotation.Autowired;
import org.springframework.ws.server.endpoint.annotation.
Endpoint;
import org.springframework.ws.server.endpoint.annotation.
PayloadRoot;
import org.springframework.ws.server.endpoint.annotation.
RequestPayload;

@Endpoint
public class CourseEndpoint {

    private XPathExpression<Element> numberExpression;

    private XPathExpression<Element> titleExpression;

    private XPathExpression<Element> subtitleExpression;

    private XPathExpression<Element> descriptionExpression;
```

```
@Autowired
public CourseEndpoint() throws JDOMException {
    Namespace namespace = Namespace.getNamespace("my",
      "http://mycompany.com/my/schemas");                  //1
    XPathFactory xPathFactory = XPathFactory.instance();
    numberExpression = xPathFactory.compile("//
    my:Number", Filters.element(), null, namespace);     //2
    titleExpression = xPathFactory.compile("//my:Title",
    Filters.element(), null, namespace);
    subtitleExpression = xPathFactory.compile
    ("//my:Subtitle", Filters.element(), null, namespace);
    descriptionExpression = xPathFactory.compile("//my:
    Description", Filters.element(), null, namespace);
}

@PayloadRoot(namespace = "http://mycompany.com/my/schemas",
                        localPart = "CourseRequest")  //3
public void handleRequest(@RequestPayload Element
courseRequest) throws Exception {
    Long number = Long.parseLong(numberExpression.
    evaluateFirst(courseRequest).getText());
    String description = descriptionExpression.
    evaluateFirst(courseRequest).getText();
    String fullTitle = titleExpression.
    evaluateFirst(courseRequest).getText() + ":"
            + subtitleExpression.
            evaluateFirst(courseRequest).getText();

    // handleCourse(number, fullTitle, description)
}

}
```

1. Since we are using JDOM2, we define the Namespace
    to be used in the Xpath definitions.

2. We define the XPathExpression instances we will
    use later to evaluate parts of the XML payload.

3. We use @PayloadRoot to define the namespace and
    element of the SOAP payload we want to match with
    this method. The @RequestPayload annotation
    on the Element parameter gets injected with the
    matched payload which we can then process in this
    method.

Generating the WSDL

Here is how we define WSDL generation within XML configuration:

```
<sws:dynamic-wsdl id="courses"
    portTypeName="CourseResource"
    locationUri="/courseService/"
    targetNamespace="http://mycompany.com/definitions">
  <sws:xsd location="/WEB-INF/my.xsd"/>
</sws:dynamic-wsdl>
```

1. First, the id determines the name of the wsdl
    resource (courses.wsdl) in this case.

2. The portTypeName determines the name of the
    WSDL port type.

3. The locationUri describes the relative location of the
    service itself.

4. The targetNamespace is optional, but defines the
    namespace within the WSDL itself.

EndpointMappings and EndpointExceptionResolvers

Spring-WS (through the `WsConfigurationSupport` class) registers the following EndpointMappings by default:

- `PayloadRootAnnotationMethodEndpointMapping` ordered at 0 for mapping requests to `@PayloadRoot` annotated controller methods

- `SoapActionAnnotationMethodEndpointMapping` ordered at 1 for mapping requests to `@SoapAction` annotated controller methods

- `AnnotationActionEndpointMapping` ordered at 2 for mapping requests to `@Action` annotated controller methods

It also registers one `EndpointAdapter`, the `DefaultMethodEndpointAdapter`, for processing requests with annotated endpoint methods and the following EndpointExceptionResolvers:

- `SoapFaultAnnotationExceptionResolver` for handling exceptions annotated with `@SoapFault`

- `SimpleSoapExceptionResolver` for creating default exceptions

Customizing

You can customize the Spring-WS configuration by implementing the WsConfigurer interface or by extending the WsConfigurerAdapter base class and overriding individual methods, for example:

Listing 10-2. CustomWsConfiguration.java

```
@Configuration
@EnableWs
@ComponentScan
public class CustomWsConfiguration extends WsConfigurerAdapter
{
    @Override
    public void addInterceptors(List<EndpointInterceptor>
    interceptors)  {
        interceptors.add(new MyInterceptor());
    }

    @Override
    public void addArgumentResolvers(
        List<MethodArgumentResolver> argumentResolvers) {
            argumentResolvers.add(myArgumentResolver());
    }

    @Bean
    public MethodArgumentResolver myArgumentResolver() {
        return new MyArgumentResolver();
    }
  }
```

WsConfigurerAdapter methods available to override:

`void addArgumentResolvers(`
`List<MethodArgumentResolver>`
`argumentResolvers)`
	Adds resolvers to support custom endpoint method argument types.

`void addInterceptors(`
`List<EndpointInterceptor>`
`interceptors)`
	Adds EndpointInterceptors for pre- and postprocessing of endpoint method invocations.

`void addReturnValueHandlers(`
`List<MethodReturnValueHandler>`
`returnValueHandlers)`
	Adds handlers to support custom controller method return value types.

EndpointInterceptor

The EndpointInterceptor interface has methods that are called for the request, response, faults, and after completion and has the ability to clear the response, modify the response, give a completely different response, or halt processing.

`void afterCompletion(`
`MessageContext messageContext,`
`Object endpoint, Exception ex)`
	Callback after completion of request and response (or fault if any) processing.

`boolean handleFault(`
`MessageContext messageContext,`
`Object endpoint)`
	Processes the outgoing response fault.

(continued)

117

`boolean handleRequest(`
`MessageContext messageContext,`
`Object endpoint)`
	Processes the incoming request message.

`boolean handleResponse(`
`MessageContext messageContext,`
`Object endpoint)`
	Processes the outgoing response message.

Each "handle" method is called as a chain, and the return value determines if processing should stop. True indicates to continue processing; false indicates to block processing at this point. If a handleRequest method returns false from any EndpointInterceptor, the endpoint itself will not be processed.

CHAPTER 11

Spring REST

REST (Representational State Transfer) outlines a way of designing web services around resources and metadata using HTTP methods like GET, POST, PUT, and PATCH to map to well-defined actions. It was first defined by Roy Fielding in his 2000 PhD dissertation "Architectural Styles and the Design of Network-based Software Architectures" at UC Irvine.[1] A web service that adheres to these principles is called *RESTful*.

This chapter is primarily about two Spring projects, Spring REST Docs and Spring HATEOAS.[2] It builds on the content from Chapter 7, so be sure to read it first before reading this chapter. Although using these projects is not required to build a RESTful web service, using them together with Spring MVC allows you to build a fully featured web API all using Spring.

---

[1]www.ics.uci.edu/~fielding/pubs/dissertation/top.htm
[2]https://spring.io/projects/spring-hateoas

© Adam L. Davis 2020
A. L. Davis, *Spring Quick Reference Guide*, https://doi.org/10.1007/978-1-4842-6144-6_11

Spring REST Docs

Spring REST Docs[3] generates documentation based on tests combined with text documents using the Asciidoctor syntax, although you may use Markdown instead. This approach is meant to generate API documents, similar to Swagger, but with more flexibility.

Spring REST Docs uses snippets produced by tests written with Spring MVC's MockMvc, Spring WebFlux's WebTestClient, or REST Assured 3.[4] This test-driven approach helps to guarantee the accuracy of your web service's documentation. If a snippet is incorrect, the test that produces it fails.

Getting Started

To get started, first add the Spring REST Docs dependency to your project. If using **Maven**, add the following dependency:

```
<dependency>
  <groupId>org.springframework.restdocs</groupId>
  <artifactId>spring-restdocs-mockmvc</artifactId>
  <version>2.0.4.RELEASE</version>
  <scope>test</scope>
</dependency>
```

---

[3]https://spring.io/projects/spring-restdocs
[4]http://rest-assured.io/

Also, add the following Maven plugin which will process the asciidoctor text during the prepare-package phase:

```
<build>
  <plugins>
  <plugin>
     <groupId>org.asciidoctor</groupId>
     <artifactId>asciidoctor-maven-plugin</artifactId>
     <version>1.5.8</version>
     <executions>
       <execution>
        <id>generate-docs</id>
        <phase>prepare-package</phase>
        <goals>

          <goal>process-asciidoc</goal>

        </goals>

        <configuration>

          <backend>html</backend>

          <doctype>book</doctype>

        </configuration>

       </execution>

     </executions>

    <dependencies>

      <dependency>

        <groupId>org.springframework.restdocs</groupId>
        <artifactId>spring-restdocs-asciidoctor</artifactId>
```

```
        <version>2.0.4.RELEASE</version>

      </dependency>

      </dependencies>

    </plugin>

  </plugins>
</build>
```

If using a **Gradle** build, use the following build file:

```
plugins {
    id "org.asciidoctor.convert" version "2.4.0"
    id "java"
}
ext {
    snippetsDir = file('build/generated-snippets')
    ver = '2.0.4.RELEASE'
}
dependencies {
asciidoctor "org.springframework.restdocs:spring-restdocs-
asciidoctor:$ver"
testCompile "org.springframework.restdocs:spring-restdocs-
mockmvc:$ver"
}
test {
    outputs.dir snippetsDir
}
asciidoctor {
    inputs.dir snippetsDir
    dependsOn test
}
```

REST Docs Generation

To generate REST Docs from an existing Spring MVC–based project, you need to write unit or integration tests for each request/response you want to document and include the JUnitRestDocumentation rule on your test.

For example, define a test using @SpringBootTest, or otherwise set up your application context in the setUp method of your test, and using @Rule, define an instance of JUnitRestDocumentation:

```
@RunWith(SpringRunner.class)
@SpringBootTest
public class GettingStartedDocumentation {
  @Rule
  public final JUnitRestDocumentation restDocumentation =
                new JUnitRestDocumentation();
```

Then set up the MockMvc instance

```
private MockMvc mockMvc;

@Before
public void setUp() {
  this.mockMvc =
  MockMvcBuilders.webAppContextSetup(this.context)
  .apply(documentationConfiguration(this.restDocumentation))
  .alwaysDo(document("{method-name}/{step}/",
        preprocessRequest(prettyPrint()),
                preprocessResponse(prettyPrint())))
        .build();
}
```

using the following static imports

```
import static org.springframework.restdocs.mockmvc.
MockMvcRestDocumentation.document;
import static
org.springframework.restdocs.mockmvc.MockMvcRestDocumentation
.documentationConfiguration;
```

For each test method within the JUnit test which uses mockMvc, Spring REST Docs will now create (during the build) a directory named by converting the test's name from CamelCase to dash-separated names (e.g., creatingACourse becomes creating-a-course) and a number-indexed directory for each HTTP request. For example, if there are four requests in a test you will have directories 1/ 2/ 3/ and 4/. Each HTTP request in turn gets the following snippets generated:

- curl-request.adoc

- httpie-request.adoc

- http-request.adoc

- http-response.adoc

- request-body.adoc

- response-body.adoc

Then, you can write the Asciidoctor documentation under the src/ docs/asciidoc/ directory and include the generated snippets into your output, for example:

```
include::{snippets}/creating-a-course/1/curl-request.adoc[]
```

```
This text is included in output.
```

```
include::{snippets}/creating-a-course/1/http-response.adoc[]
```

This would include each of the preceding snippets within your documentation output (typically HTML5 output).

Serving the Documentation in Spring Boot

To serve the HTML5 generated documentation in a Spring Boot-based project, add the following to your Gradle build file:

```
bootJar {
  dependsOn asciidoctor
  from ("${asciidoctor.outputDir}/html5") {
    into 'static/docs'
  }
}
```

Spring HATEOAS

Closely related to REST is the concept of *Hypermedia as the engine of application state* (HATEOAS),[5] which outlines how each response from a web service should provide information, or links, that describe other endpoints, much like how websites work. Spring HATEOAS[6] helps enable these types of RESTful web services.

---

[5]https://en.wikipedia.org/wiki/HATEOAS
[6]https://spring.io/projects/spring-hateoas

Getting Started

To get started, first add the Spring HATEOAS dependency to your project. If using Spring Boot and Maven, add the following dependency:

```
<dependency>
  <groupId>org.springframework.boot</groupId>
  <artifactId>spring-boot-starter-hateoas</artifactId>
</dependency>
```

If using Spring Boot with Gradle, use the following dependency:

```
implementation 'org.springframework.boot:spring-boot-starter-hateoas'
```

Creating Links

The key part of HATEOAS is the link, which can contain a URI or URI template and allows the client to easily navigate the REST API and provides for future compatibility – the client can use the link allowing the server to change where that link points.

Spring HATEOAS supplies methods for easily creating Links, such as the LinkBuilder and WebMvcLinkBuilder. It also supplies models for representing Links in the response, such as EntityModel, PagedModel, CollectionModel, and RepresentationModel. Which model to use depends on what type of data you are returning one entity (EntityModel), pages of data (PagedModel), or others.

Let's take one example using the WebMvcLinkBuilder and the EntityModel:

```
package com.apress.spring_quick.rest;

import org.springframework.hateoas.EntityModel;
import org.springframework.web.bind.annotation.GetMapping;
```

```java
import org.springframework.web.bind.annotation.RestController;

import static org.springframework.hateoas.server.mvc.
WebMvcLinkBuilder.linkTo;

@RestController
public class GettingStartedController {
    @GetMapping("/")
    public EntityModel<Customer> getCustomer() {
        return EntityModel.of(new Customer("John", "Doe"))

.add(linkTo(GettingStartedController.class).withSelfRel())

    .add(linkTo(GettingStartedController.class)

    .slash("next").withRel("next"));
    }
}
```

At runtime, this endpoint would return the following as JSON (when running locally):

```json
{
  "firstname":"John",
  "lastname":"Doe",
  "_links":{
    "self":{"href":"http://localhost:8080"},
    "next":{"href":"http://localhost:8080/next"}
  }
}
```

HYPERTEXT APPLICATION LANGUAGE

Hypertext Application Language (HAL)[7] is a draft standard for defining hypermedia such as links to external resources within JSON or XML code. The standard was initially proposed on June 2012 specifically for use with JSON and has since become available in two variations, JSON and XML. The two associated MIME types are media type: `application/hal+xml` and media type: `application/hal+json`. HAL consists of resources and links. It can have embedded resources which also have links. For example, if a Course has many tests, you might see HAL JSON like the following:

```
{
    "_links": {
        "self": { "href": "http://localhost:8080/courses" },
        "next": { "href": "http://localhost:8080/courses?page=2" },
        "my:find": {
            "href": "http://localhost:8080/courses/{?name}",
            "templated": true
        }
    },
    "total": 14,
    "_embedded": {}
}
```

Testing

Testing the HATEOAS output can be achieved similarly to testing any web service that produces XML or JSON.

---

[7]https://tools.ietf.org/html/draft-kelly-json-hal-00

In the common case where your service produces JSON, it would be helpful to use a library to navigate the JSON in a similar way to how XPath navigates XML documents, *JsonPath*. One library that implements JsonPath in Java is *Jayway JsonPath*.[8] Although you can use it directly, Spring wraps the usage of JsonPath with the static MockMvcResultMatchers.jsonPath method for ease of use with Hamcrest matchers.

To use JsonPath, we simply need to include a dependency in the Maven pom:

```
<dependency>
    <groupId>com.jayway.jsonpath</groupId>
    <artifactId>json-path</artifactId>
    <version>2.4.0</version>
    <scope>test</scope>
</dependency>
```

Or if using Gradle, include

```
testCompile 'com.jayway.jsonpath:json-path:2.4.0'
```

For example, see the following JUnit test class which uses JsonPath to validate that _links.self and _links.next are not null:

Listing 11-1. GettingStartedDocumentation.java

```
import org.junit.jupiter.api.BeforeEach;
import org.junit.jupiter.api.Test;
import org.junit.jupiter.api.extension.ExtendWith;
import org.springframework.beans.factory.annotation.Autowired;
import org.springframework.boot.test.context.SpringBootTest;
```

---

[8]https://github.com/json-path/JsonPath

```
import org.springframework.hateoas.MediaTypes;
import org.springframework.test.context.junit.jupiter.
SpringExtension;
import org.springframework.test.web.servlet.MockMvc;
import org.springframework.test.web.servlet.setup.
MockMvcBuilders;
import org.springframework.web.context.WebApplicationContext;

import static org.springframework.test.web.servlet.request.
MockMvcRequestBuilders.*;
import static org.springframework.test.web.servlet.result.
MockMvcResultMatchers.*;
import static org.hamcrest.Matchers.*;

@ExtendWith(SpringExtension.class) // JUnit 5
@SpringBootTest
public class GettingStartedDocumentation {

  @Autowired
  private WebApplicationContext context;

  private MockMvc mockMvc;

  @BeforeEach
  public void setUp() {
    this.mockMvc = MockMvcBuilders.webAppContextSetup
    (this.context)
        .build();
  }
```

```
@Test
public void index() throws Exception {
  this.mockMvc.perform(get("/").accept(MediaTypes.HAL_JSON))
      .andExpect(status().isOk())
      .andExpect(jsonPath("_links.self", is(notNullValue())))
      .andExpect(jsonPath("_links.next", is(notNullValue())));
 }
}
```

CHAPTER 12

Reactor

Reactor[1] is Spring's implementation of reactive streams (in version 3 and beyond). It has two main publisher types, `Flux<T>` and `Mono<T>`. It uses Schedulers to determine on which thread to run each operation.

The Spring framework integrates in many ways with Reactor to make it easier to use with other Spring projects such as Spring Data and Spring Security. Spring WebFlux is a web framework much like Spring MVC but built around reactive streams and capable of running on Netty, a nonblocking I/O client-server framework.

Why Use Reactor?

The purpose of Reactor, and reactive streams in general, is to enable operations on large amounts of data to be broken down and executed on many different threads (multithreading) in the most efficient, scalable, and fast way possible. Although parallel processing can be achieved simply using Java 8's parallel stream, reactive streams add a plethora of additional functionality and customization such as error handling, retry, caching and replaying streams, handling backpressure, and more.

---

[1]`https://projectreactor.io/`

© Adam L. Davis 2020
A. L. Davis, *Spring Quick Reference Guide*, https://doi.org/10.1007/978-1-4842-6144-6_12

You can think of a reactive stream as having three rails, the data rail, the completion rail (whether or not the stream has completed), and the error rail. Also, each of the rails can be converted into the other: complete streams could be replaced, an operation could throw an Exception, or an Exception could be handled and replaced with more data.

In addition, Reactor adds the concept of Context, which we will explore later on in this chapter.

Getting Started

If you have a Maven build, add the following to your pom file:

```
<dependency>
  <groupId>io.projectreactor</groupId>
  <artifactId>reactor-core</artifactId>
  <version>3.3.7.RELEASE</version>
</dependency>
<dependency>
  <groupId>io.projectreactor</groupId>
  <artifactId>reactor-test</artifactId>
  <version>3.3.7.RELEASE</version>
  <scope>test</scope>
</dependency>
```

For Gradle builds, add the following to your Gradle build file's dependencies:

```
implementation 'io.projectreactor:reactor-core:3.3.7.RELEASE'
testImplementation 'io.projectreactor:reactor-
test:3.3.7.RELEASE'
```

Flux

Flux<T> is the main entry point for Reactor reactive streams.[2] Mono<T> is like a Flux<T> but for zero or one element. Both Mono<T> and Flux<T> implement org.reactivestreams.Publisher<T>.

```
import reactor.core.publisher.Flux;
import reactor.core.publisher.Mono;
```

Like any reactive streams implementation, Reactor uses Schedulers to decide on which thread to run for each operation.

```
Flux.range(1, 100)
  .publishOn(Schedulers.parallel())
  .subscribe(v -> doSomething(v));
```

Handling errors in Reactor is achieved through method calls on the stream. The following methods may be used on a Flux<T> or Mono<T> (generic types omitted for brevity):

- onErrorResume(Function) – Takes the Exception and returns a different Publisher as a fallback or secondary stream

- onErrorMap(Function) – Takes the Exception and allows you to modify it or return a completely new Exception if you prefer

- onErrorReturn(T) – Provides a default value to use when an error arises

- doOnError(Consumer<? extends Throwable>) – Allows you to handle the error without affecting the underlying stream in any way

---

[2]A Flux is similar to a Flowable or Observable from RxJava if you are familiar.

Errors (thrown Exceptions) are always ending events for a Flux and should be handled by a Subscriber. However, many times, such as in the preceding example, an error is not possible and therefore does not need to be handled.

Mono

Why have a separate class, called Mono, just one or zero elements? Think of it like a translation of Java 8's Optional class into the Reactive Streams world.

Mono is very similar to Flux except that it has methods like

- `justOrEmpty(T)` – Takes a nullable value and converts into a Mono. If null, the result is the same as Mono. empty().

- `justOrEmpty(Optional<? extends T>)` – Takes an Optional and converts into a Mono directly.

Unlike Java's Optional, Mono can handle errors, among other things. For example, a method that returns Mono might do the following:

```
return Mono.error(new RuntimeException("your error"))
```

The corresponding code can handle errors from a Mono in the same way as with a Flux (using onErrorResume, onErrorMap, or onErrorReturn).

Creating a Flux or Mono

You can create a Flux from fixed data (cold) or programmatically from dynamic data (hot).

The following are some different ways to create a cold Flux:

```
Flux<String> flux1 = Flux.just("a", "b", "foobar");        //1
List<String> iterable = Arrays.asList("a", "b", "foobar");
Flux<String> flux2 = Flux.fromIterable(iterable);          //2
Flux<Integer> numbers = Flux.range(1, 64);                 //3
```

1. Create a Flux from a list of values.

2. Create a Flux from an iterable.

3. Create a range from 1 to 64.

You can create a simple Mono that is empty or has just one element like the following:

```
Mono<String> noData = Mono.empty();    //1
Mono<String> data = Mono.just("foo"); //2
Mono<String> monoError = Mono.error(new
RuntimeException("error")); //3
```

1. Create an empty Mono.

2. Create a Mono with one element.

3. Create a Mono wrapping a RuntimeException.

You can programmatically create a Flux using one of the generate, create, or push methods.

The generate method has multiple overloaded definitions, but for simplicity let's focus on the one that takes a Supplier and a BiFunction. The function takes as parameters the current state and a SynchronousSink which can be used to publish the next state of the stream. For example, the following uses an AtomicLong instance to increment the numbers 0 through 10 and supplies the square of each number:

```
Flux<Long> squares = Flux.generate(
  AtomicLong::new, //1
  (state, sink) -> {
    long i = state.getAndIncrement();
    sink.next(i * i); //2
    if (i == 10) sink.complete(); //3
    return state;
});
```

1. The constructor of AtomicLong is used as the
    supplier.

2. After incrementing, supply the square of the number
    to the sink.

3. After 10, the complete is called, which calls
    onComplete to any subscriber, closing out the Flux.
    The create method exposes a FluxSink with next,
    error, and complete methods. This allows you to
    arbitrarily publish data onto a Flux.

For example, the following demonstrates registering a MessageListener
which handles a list of messages:

```
Flux<String> bridge = Flux.create(sink -> {
 messageProcessor.register(
  new MessageListener<String>() {
  public void handle(List<String> chunks) {
  for(String s : chunks) {
   sink.next(s);
  }
 }
```

```
public void processComplete() {
 sink.complete();
 }
public void processError(Throwable e) {
 sink.error(e);
 }
});
});
```

If the messages processed here have a single-threaded source, the push method can be used instead of *create*.

Schedulers

The Schedulers class under the reactor.core.scheduler package provides many static methods for providing Schedulers that determine on which Thread or Threads your code will run.

The following are some of those static methods and their meaning:

- Schedulers.immediate() – The current thread.

- Schedulers.single() – A single, reusable thread. Note that this method reuses the same thread for all callers, until the Scheduler is disposed. If you want a per-call dedicated thread, use Schedulers.newSingle() for each call.

- Schedulers.elastic() – An elastic thread pool. It creates new worker pools as needed and reuses idle ones. Worker pools that stay idle for too long (default is 60 seconds) are disposed. This is a good choice for I/O blocking work, for instance. Schedulers.elastic() is a handy way to give a blocking process its own thread, so that it does not tie up other resources.

- Schedulers.parallel() – A fixed pool of workers. It creates as many workers as you have CPU cores.

- Schedulers.fromExecutor(Executor) – Creates a Scheduler to use the given Executor, allowing you to use your extensive knowledge of Java's Executors.

For example, let's take our example of generating squares and make it run in parallel:

```
List<Integer> squares = new ArrayList<>();
Flux.range(1, 64).flatMap(v -> // 1
Mono.just(v)
 .subscribeOn(Schedulers.newSingle("comp"))          //2
 .map(w -> w * w))
 .doOnError(ex -> ex.printStackTrace())                //3
 .doOnComplete(() -> System.out.println("Completed")) //4
 .subscribeOn(Schedulers.immediate())
 .subscribe(squares::add);                             //5
```

1. First, we use Flux.range to take the range from 1 to 64 and call flatMap (which takes a lambda expression that converts each value in the range into a new Reactor type, Mono in this case).

2. Using Schedulers.newSingle(name), we create a new single thread for each value, and passing to subscribeOn will cause the mapping expression to be executed on that single thread. Keep in mind we are describing the execution of the Mono here, not the initial Flux.

3. We provide exception handling code using doOnError just in case.

4. Using doOnComplete, we print out "Completed" when the whole execution is finished.

5. Finally, we subscribe to the Flux (without this step, nothing would ever happen) and add the result to our list of squares.

Here we see once again how in Reactive Streams, everything can become a Stream, even a single value. By creating a Mono for each value in the range, we're able to use Reactor to declare what kind of threading we want for every calculation. In this case, since we use newSingle, all of the processing will be done in parallel with a new thread for each of the 64 values.

However, this is probably not the most efficient implementation since creating lots of Threads causes a lot of overhead. Instead, we should use Schedulers.parallel() so that the exact number of Threads your CPU can handle will be created. In this way, Reactor takes care of the details for you.

Pull Events

If you have more of a "pull" situation (events are created by polling a source), you can use the onRequest method of FluxSink<T>. For example, the following code creates a Flux that polls a channel for new events:

```
Flux<String> bridge = Flux.create(sink -> {
sink.onRequest(n -> channel.poll(n)) // 1
  .onCancel(channel::cancel)          // 2
  .onDispose(channel::close);         // 3
  channel.register(sink::next);       // 4
});
```

1. Poll for events from the channel when requests are made with the given number. This "n" is the number of items requested.

2. Call the channel's `cancel` method when the Flux is canceled.

3. The `channel.close()` method is given to `onDispose` to be invoked for complete, error, or cancel.

4. Finally, register the sink's `next` method as a listener to the channel.

Keep in mind that onRequest will not be called multiple times for no reason. Reactor is very precise.

It will call onRequest with some number (such as 32) and then not call it again until a significant number of items have been published to the Flux (i.e., after sink.next is called 32 times).

ℹ The code examples used in this chapter are available online.[3]

Handling Backpressure

Reactor, like all implementations of Reactive Streams, has the ability to handle backpressure. Simply use one of the following methods on a Flux (or others not listed) to specify which backpressure strategy you want to use:

- onBackpressureBuffer() – Buffers all items until they can be handled downstream.

- onBackpressureBuffer(maxSize) – Buffers items up to the given count.

---

[3]https://github.com/adamldavis/spring-quick-ref

- onBackpressureBuffer(maxSize, BufferOverflow Strategy) – Buffers items up to the given count and allows you to specify the BufferOverflowStrategy, such as onBackpressureBuffer(100, BufferOverflowStrategy. DROP_OLDEST).

- onBackpressureLatest() – Similar to keeping a buffer of only the last item added. If the downstream does not keep up with the upstream, only the latest element will be given downstream.

- onBackpressureError() – Ends the Flux with an error (calling the downstream Subscriber's onError) with an IllegalStateException from Exceptions. failWithOverflow() if more items were produced upstream than requested downstream.

- onBackpressureDrop() – Drops any items produced above what was requested.

- onBackpressureDrop(Consumer) – Drops any items produced above what was requested and calls the given Consumer for each dropped item.

With each of these methods, the strategy only applies when items are produced on the stream faster than they can be handled by the downstream (subscriber). If that's not the case, for example, with a cold stream, no backpressure strategy is necessary.

Also keep in mind that Reactor is not magic, and some care should be taken when considering backpressure strategies.

> ℹ Backpressure is what happens when there are too many events/ data in a stream than the downstream can handle. As an analogy, think of what happens in some cities at rush hour when traffic grinds to a halt – or when subway trains are filled to capacity. Backpressure is a feedback mechanism to slow it down.[4]

Context

Reactor comes with an advanced feature that is somewhat comparable to ThreadLocal but applied to a Flux or a Mono instead of a Thread: the Context.

Reactor's Context is much like an immutable Map or key/value store. It is stored transparently from the Subscriber upward through the Subscription.

Context is Reactor specific and does not work with the other Reactive Streams implementations.

When setting up the Context, you should not define it toward the beginning of the Flux. For example, do not do this (the Context will not be available downstream as you might expect):

```
// this is WRONG!
Flux<Integer> flux = Flux.just(1).subscriberContext(Context.
of("pid", 12));
```

---

[4]https://reactivemanifesto.org/glossary#Back-Pressure

Instead, you should define it toward the end since it propagates "backward" up the chain, for example:

```
Flux<Integer> flux = Flux.just(1);
Flux<String> stringFlux = flux.flatMap(i ->
Mono.subscriberContext().map(ctx -> i + " pid: " +
                         ctx.getOrDefault("pid", 0)));
// supply context here:
StepVerifier.create(stringFlux.subscriberContext(Context.
of("pid", 123)))
  .expectNext("1 pid: 123")
  .verifyComplete();
```

The preceding code uses the **StepVerifier** (which we cover next) to verify that we get the expected value.

Note how we use the static method on Mono, `Mono.subscriberContext()`, to access the Context.

ⓘ Reactor has excellent online documentation.[5]

Testing

Automated testing is always a good idea, and it would be nice to have tools to directly test Reactive Streams. Luckily, Reactor comes with a few elements dedicated to testing which are gathered into their own artifact we included at the beginning of this chapter: reactor-test.

---

[5]`https://projectreactor.io/docs`

The two main uses of reactor-test are the following:

- Testing that a sequence follows a given scenario with StepVerifier

- Producing data in order to test the behavior of operators (including your own operators) downstream with TestPublisher.

StepVerifier

Reactor's StepVerifier can be used to verify the behavior of a Reactor Publisher (Flux or Mono).

Here's a simple example of a JUnit test utilizing StepVerifier:

```
@Test
public void testStepVerifier_Mono_error() {
  Mono<String> monoError = Mono.error(new
RuntimeException("error")); //1
  StepVerifier.create(monoError) //2
    .expectErrorMessage("error") //3
    .verify(); //4
}
```

1. Create a Mono wrapping a RuntimeException imitating an actual error state.

2. Create a StepVerifier wrapping that Mono.

3. Declare that an onError event is expected and the Exception's error message is "error".

4. We call verify() at the end. This will throw an AssertionError if any expectations are not met.

Next, we'll create a Mono of just one string and verify it:

```
@Test public void testStepVerifier_Mono_foo() {
  Mono<String> foo = Mono.just("foo"); //1
  StepVerifier.create(foo)                   //2
    .expectNext("foo")                       //3
    .verifyComplete();                       //4
}
```

1. Create a Mono wrapping one value, "foo".

2. Create a StepVerifier wrapping that Mono.

3. Expect onNext is called with "foo".

4. Calling verifyComplete() has the same effect as verify() but also expects onComplete was called.

Here, we will test a Flux with three values and timeout if it takes too long:

```
@Test public void testStepVerifier_Flux() {
  Flux<Integer> flux = Flux.just(1, 4, 9); //1
  StepVerifier.create(flux)                   //2
    .expectNext(1)                            //3
    .expectNext(4)
    .expectNext(9)
    .expectComplete()                         //4
    .verify(Duration.ofSeconds(10));          //5
}
```

1. Create a Flux of just three numbers.

2. Create a StepVerifier wrapping that Flux.

3. Call expectNext for each value expected.

4. Call expectComplete to expect onComplete to be called.

5. Finally, you must call verify() at the end. This variation of verify takes a Duration timeout value. Here, it is 10 seconds. This can be useful to prevent the Test from hanging in cases where a Publisher might never call onComplete.

TestPublisher

The TestPublisher<T> class offers the ability to provide finely tuned data for test purposes. TestPublisher<T> is a reactive streams Publisher<T> but can be converted to either a Flux or Mono using flux() or mono() methods.

TextPublisher has the following methods:

- next(T) and next(T, T...) – Triggers 1-n onNext signals

- emit(T...) - Does the same as next and also terminates with an onComplete signal

- complete() – Terminates with an onComplete signal

- error(Throwable) – Terminates with an onError signal.

The following demonstrates how you might use TestPublisher<T>:

```
TestPublisher<Object> publisher = TestPublisher.create(); //1
Flux<Object> stringFlux = publisher.flux();                //2
List list = new ArrayList();                               //3
stringFlux.subscribe(next -> list.add(next),
                     ex -> ex.printStackTrace());          //4
publisher.emit("foo", "bar");                              //5
assertEquals(2, list.size());                              //6
assertEquals("foo", list.get(0));
assertEquals("bar", list.get(1));
```

1. Create the TestPublisher instance.

2. Convert it to a Flux.

3. Create a new List. For test purposes, we will use this list to collect values from the publisher.

4. Subscribe to the publisher using two lambda expressions for onNext and onError. This will add each value emitted from the publisher to the list.

5. Finally, emit the values "foo" and "bar" from the TestPublisher.

6. Assert the list's size is two as expected.

Note that you must subscribe to the `TestPublisher` (which is done by subscribing to the `stringFlux` in the preceding example) before emitting any values.

Tuples and Zip

Tuples are strongly typed collections of two or more elements, and Reactor comes with them built-in. Some operations such as `zipWith` return reactive streams of Tuples.

Flux has an instance method `zipWith(Publisher<? extends T2> source2)` which has a return type of `Flux<Tuple2<T,T2>>`. It waits for both Fluxes (the initial flux and source2) to emit an element and then combines the two into a Tuple2. There's also a static method Flux.zip which is overloaded to take from two to eight Publishers and zip them together into Tuples.

Zipping is useful when you want to perform multiple operations that return reactive results (Flux or Mono) and combine them.

Mono has two main flavors of zipping (nonstatic methods which both have a return type of `Mono<Tuple2<T,T2>>`):

- `zipWith(Mono<? extends T2> other)` – Zips the current stream with another stream, giving the combination of each corresponding element in the form of Tuple2.

- `zipWhen(Function<T,Mono<? extends T2>> rightGenerator)` – Zips the current Mono with another Mono, giving the combination of each corresponding element in the form of Tuple2, but only after the first stream's operation has completed, thus allowing you to use the result of the first Mono to produce the second Mono.

For example, given you have two methods which perform asynchronous operations Mono<Course> getCourse(Long id) and Mono<Integer> getStudentCount(Course course), imagine you want to get the student count from the course Id, you could do the following:

```
Mono<Integer>  getStudentCount(Long id) {
  return getCourse(id)
    .zipWhen(course -> getStudentCount(course))
    .map(tuple2 -> tuple2.getT2());
}
```

This is a simple example, but you can imagine combining two different entities, or performing logic on them before returning, or calling another method which takes two arguments, and so on.

Reactor Addons

Project Reactor provides additional functionality under the `io.projectreactor.addons` groupId. Reactor extra includes additional math functions, different ways to retry including Jitter and Backoff, and TupleUtils.

```
<dependency>
    <groupId>io.projectreactor.addons</groupId>
    <artifactId>reactor-extra</artifactId>
    <version>3.3.3.RELEASE</version>
</dependency>
```

For Gradle builds, add the following to your Gradle build file's dependencies:

```
implementation 'io.projectreactor.addons:reactor-extra:3.3.3.RELEASE'
```

When your application fails at an integration point, such as when calling another RESTful service, to make your overall system reliable, you might want to retry the call some number of times. However, to keep from overloading the failing service, you should employ Backoff, or increasing the time between each retry, and Jitter, randomly modifying the time so that the retries from many different instances do not happen at the same time (correlate). For example, take a look at the following code:

```
var retry = Retry.anyOf(IOException.class)              \\1
        .exponentialBackoff(Duration.ofMillis(100),     \\2
                    Duration.ofSeconds(60))
        .jitter(Jitter.random())                        \\3
        .retryMax(5)
        .withApplicationContext(appContext)             \\4
        .doOnRetry(context ->
            context.applicationContext().rollback());
    return flux.retryWhen(retry);                       \\5
```

151

1. We create the Retry with an exception value of IOException, meaning it will retry only when that exception is thrown (any Exception class or classes could be provided here; the example is only IOException).

2. We define exponential backoff with a starting value of 100 ms and maximum value of 60 seconds.

3. We add random Jitter and set the retry max to 5, meaning it retries at most five times.

4. We add the Spring ApplicationContext and use it to apply rollback after each failure.

5. Finally, we call retryWhen(retry) on a Flux instance to apply the Retry to that Flux.

ⓘ For more information on retries, backoff, and jitter, see this excellent article from The Amazon Builders' Library.[6]

---

[6]https://aws.amazon.com/builders-library/timeouts-retries-and-backoff-with-jitter/

CHAPTER 13

Spring Integration

Spring Integration is a programming model to support the well-known enterprise integration patterns.

Features

Spring Integration implements many common enterprise integration patterns,[1] such as Channel, Aggregator, Filter, and Transformer, and provides an abstraction over many different messaging implementations.

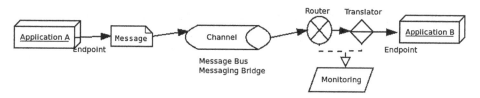

Figure 13-1. *Enterprise Integration*

Spring Integration provides a messaging paradigm to separate an application into components that communicate without knowing about each other. In addition to wiring together fine-grained components, Spring Integration provides many channel adapters and gateways to communicate with external systems. Channel adapters are used for one-way integration (send or receive), and gateways are used for request/reply scenarios (inbound or outbound).

---

[1]www.enterpriseintegrationpatterns.com/

Messaging supported includes but is not limited to

- REST/HTTP

- FTP/SFTP

- Twitter

- Web Services (SOAP)

- TCP/UDP

- JMS

- RabbitMQ

- Email

ℹ Spring Cloud Integration

The *Spring Cloud Stream* project builds on Spring Integration, where Spring Integration is used as an engine for message-driven microservices. This is covered in Chapter 18.

Getting Started

The easiest way to get started is using the Spring Initializr or Spring Boot CLI to create a new project (they are covered in Chapter 15). In an existing project, add the following dependencies:

```
implementation 'org.springframework.boot:spring-boot-starter-
integration'
testImplementation 'org.springframework.integration:spring-
integration-test'
```

Then also include any other Spring Boot starters or other libraries you will need for your project, for example:

```
implementation 'org.springframework.boot:spring-boot-starter-amqp'
testImplementation 'org.springframework.amqp:spring-rabbit-test'
```

This brings in the Spring Boot starter for AMQP and spring-rabbit-test for testing integration with RabbitMQ.

Then, in a Spring Boot application, add the @EnableIntegration annotation to one of your configuration classes which does the following:

- Registers some built-in beans, such as errorChannel and its LoggingHandler, taskScheduler for pollers, jsonPath SpEL-function, and others.

- Adds several BeanFactoryPostProcessor instances.

- Adds several BeanPostProcessor instances to enhance or convert and wrap particular beans for integration purposes.

- Adds annotation processors to parse messaging annotations and registers components for them with the application context.

You can also use @IntegrationComponentScan to scan the classpath for Spring Integration–specific annotations such as the @MessagingGateway annotation.

Putting it all together, your main application class might look like the following:

```
@EnableIntegration
@IntegrationComponentScan
@SpringBootApplication
public class SpringIntApplication {
```

```
public static void main(String[] args) {
        SpringApplication.run(SpringIntApplication.
        class, args);
    }
}
```

Adding Additional Support

In general, when you want to use Spring Integration with a particular technology, such as JPA, you include the additional artifact named spring-integration-*X* under the org.springframework.integration groupId, for example, for Kafka:[2]

```
<dependency>
    <groupId>org.springframework.integration</groupId>
    <artifactId>spring-integration-kafka</artifactId>
    <version>3.3.0.RELEASE</version>
</dependency>
```

Some of the available supports:

JPA	HTTP	JDBC	JMS
Mail	MongoDB	Kafka	Redis
Resource	RMI	RSocket	SFTP
STOMP	Stream	Syslog	TCP and UDP (ip)
WebFlux	Web Services	XML	XMPP

---

[2]https://kafka.apache.org/quickstart

Message Gateway

A Message Gateway is the abstraction Spring Integration used over an existing messaging technology which allows your code to interact with an interface without needing to know about the underlying channel. When you annotate an interface with @MessagingGateway and annotate one or more methods with @Gateway annotations, Spring implements the interface with a proxy at runtime using the underlying technology from the support artifact you included.

For example, for a Kafka Message Gateway:

```
//Use the following imports:
import org.springframework.messaging.Message;
import org.springframework.messaging.handler.annotation.Header;
import org.springframework.integration.annotation.
MessagingGateway;
import org.springframework.integration.annotation.Gateway;
import org.springframework.kafka.support.KafkaHeaders;
@MessagingGateway
public interface KafkaGateway {
    @Gateway(requestChannel = "toKafka.input")            \\1
    void sendToKafka(String payload,
                    @Header(KafkaHeaders.TOPIC) String
                    topic);                               \\2

    @Gateway(replyChannel = "fromKafka",
    replyTimeout = 10000)  \\3
    Message<?> receiveFromKafka();
}
```

1. Define the requestChannel to send data, in this case, a String payload.

2. Using @Header defines a header, in this case, the Kafka topic the message payload will be sent to.

3. Define the replyChannel, which can be used to get messages from Kafka. Note the return type is Spring's Message<T> interface, an abstraction which can be used for any messaging system. The replyTimeout is in milliseconds, so here it is ten seconds.

Assuming everything is set up correctly, Spring Integration implements the KafkaGateway interface as a Spring Bean at runtime, so it can be invoked in the following way:

```
KafkaGateway kafkaGateway = context.getBean(KafkaGateway.class);
String message = "any message";
String topic = "topic";
kafkaGateway.sendToKafka(message, topic);
```

IntegrationFlow

There are two main ways to create flows (implementing the IntegrationFlow interface), either using a lambda expression or using the fluent builder DSL starting with the IntegrationFlows class.

In the first instance, we are taking advantage of the fact that IntegrationFlow is a SAM (Single Abstract Method) interface, so a lambda expression with one parameter can be supplied, and Java will know it implements the interface from the return type, for example:

```
@Bean
public IntegrationFlow toKafka(KafkaTemplate<?, ?>
kafkaTemplate) {
    return flowDefinition -> flowDefinition
            .handle(Kafka.outboundChannelAdapter
            (kafkaTemplate)
                    .messageKey("si.key"));
}
```

The IntegrationFlows class can be used to create an IntegrationFlow, for example:

```
@Bean
public IntegrationFlow fromKafkaFlow(
                ConsumerFactory<?, ?> consumerFactory) {
    return IntegrationFlows
      .from(Kafka.messageDrivenChannelAdapter
      (consumerFactory, topic))
      .channel((Channels c) -> c.queue("fromKafka"))
      .get();
}
```

The IntegrationFlows.from static method returns an IntegrationFlowBuilder which extends IntegrationFlowDefinition and has the "get()" method which returns a new instance of StandardIntegrationFlow. The methods on IntegrationFlowDefinition allow you to fluently build an IntegrationFlow and include the following:

- aggregate – Aggregator-specific implementation of AbstractCorrelatingMessageHandler, a message handler that holds a buffer of correlated messages in a MessageStore. It takes care of correlated groups of messages that can be completed in batches.

- barrier – A message handler that suspends the thread until a message with corresponding correlation is passed into the trigger method or the timeout occurs.

- bridge – A simple MessageHandler implementation that passes the request Message directly to the output channel without modifying it. The main purpose of this handler is to bridge a PollableChannel to a SubscribableChannel or vice versa.

- channel – Defines methods for sending messages.

- claimCheckIn – Populates the MessageTransforming Handler for the ClaimCheckInTransformer with the provided MessageStore.

- claimCheckOut – Populates the MessageTransformingHandler for the ClaimCheckOutTransformer with the provided MessageStore.

- controlBus – Populates the Control Bus EI Pattern-specific MessageHandler implementation at the current IntegrationFlow chain position.

- convert – Populates the MessageTransformingHandler instance for the provided payloadType to convert at runtime.

- delay – Populates a DelayHandler to the current integration flow position.

- enrich – Populates a ContentEnricher to the current integration flow position with provided options. ContentEnricher is a Message Transformer that can augment a message's payload with either dynamic or static values.

- enrichHeaders – Populates a MessageTransformingHandler that adds statically configured header values to a Message.

- filter – A MessageFilter only passes to filter's output channel if the message passes a given MessageSelector.

- fixedSubscriberChannel – Populates an instance of FixedSubscriberChannel (a specialized SubscribableChannel for a single final subscriber set up during bean instantiation) at the current IntegrationFlow chain position.

- fluxTransform – Populates a FluxMessageChannel to start a reactive processing for upstream data, wrap it to a Flux, apply the provided Function via Flux. transform(Function), and emit the result to one more FluxMessageChannel, subscribed in the downstream flow.

- gateway – Populates the "artificial" GatewayMessageHandler for the provided subflow or channel.

- handle – Populates a ServiceActivatingHandler for the provided MessageHandler or MessageProcessorSpec bean and method-name.

- headerFilter – Provides the HeaderFilter to the current StandardIntegrationFlow.

- log – Populates a WireTap for the current message channel and uses a LoggingHandler, a MessageHandler implementation that simply logs the Message or its payload.

- logAndReply – This operator can be used only in the end of the flow. Does the same as "log" method. Returns `IntegrationFlow`.

- nullChannel – Adds a bean into this flow definition as a terminal operator. Returns `IntegrationFlow`.

- publishSubscribeChannel – The `PublishSubscribe Channel` (a channel that sends Messages to each of its subscribers) `BaseIntegrationFlowDefinition`. `channel(java.lang.String)` method-specific implementation to allow the use of the "subflow" subscriber capability.

- resequence – Populates a ResequencingMessageHandler, which resequences messages, using a buffer of correlated messages in a MessageStore.

- route – Many different variations of this method exist. They populate the MethodInvokingRouter, or an ExpressionEvaluatingRouter if provided a SpEL expression, which then determines a MessageChannel or channel name to use.

- routeByException – Can route messages by Exception type.

- routeToRecipients – Populates the RecipientListRouter with options from the RecipientListRouterSpec, which sends messages on multiple channels.

- scatterGather – Populates a ScatterGatherHandler to the current integration flow position based on the provided MessageChannel for scattering function and AggregatorSpec for gathering function.

- split – Populates either the MethodInvokingSplitter to evaluate the provided method of the service at runtime or the ExpressionEvaluatingSplitter with the provided SpEL expression. A splitter splits message into multiple Messages.

- transform – Populates the MessageTransformingHandler instance for the provided GenericTransformer.

- trigger – Populates a ServiceActivatingHandler instance to perform MessageTriggerAction.

- wireTap – Populates the Wire Tap EI Pattern-specific ChannelInterceptor implementation to the currentMessageChannel.

This is by no means exhaustive. Most of these methods have several overloaded variations.

Kafka Config

You can then configure the Spring Integration Kafka-specific settings in application.yml under spring.kafka.consumer and spring.kafka. producer, for example:

Listing 13-1. application.yml

```
spring:
  kafka:
    consumer:
      group-id: siTestGroup
      auto-offset-reset: earliest
      enable-auto-commit: false
```

```
    value-deserializer: org.apache.kafka.common.
    serialization.StringDeserializer
    key-deserializer: org.apache.kafka.common.serialization.
    StringDeserializer
  producer:
    batch-size: 16384
    buffer-memory: 33554432
    retries: 0
    key-serializer: org.apache.kafka.common.serialization.
    StringSerializer
    value-serializer: org.apache.kafka.common.serialization.
    StringSerializer
```

✏️ Installing Kafka is left as an exercise for the reader. Go to `https://kafka.apache.org/quickstart` and follow the instructions. Then follow the content of this chapter to set up Spring Integration.

Topics

Since we are using Kafka, we also need to create the topics initially.

Since we're using Spring Boot with auto-configuration, Spring Boot's auto-configured KafkaAdmin (from `spring-integration-kafka`) will provision the topics for us if we provide NewTopic Spring Beans, for example:

```
@Bean
public NewTopic topic() {
    return new NewTopic("topic", 5, (short) 1);
}
```

```
@Bean
public NewTopic newTopic() {
    return new NewTopic("topic2", 5, (short) 1);
}
```

This would create two topics named "topic" and "topic2" with replication of 1 (meaning only one copy is stored) and 5 partitions, meaning the data will be split into five partitions.

Monitoring

By default, if a Micrometer `meterRegistry` bean is present, which will be the case in a Spring Boot project with Spring Actuator included, Spring Integration metrics will be managed by Micrometer. If you wish to use legacy Spring Integration metrics, add a `DefaultMetricsFactory` (from Spring Integration) bean to the application context.

CHAPTER 14

Spring Batch

Spring Batch is a project to support long-running data conversion or similar long-running processes for enterprise systems. It has tons of features, some of which we will cover.

Features

Spring Batch provides features for partitioning and processing high volumes of data. It also provides reusable functions that are essential in processing large volumes of records, including transaction management, job processing statistics, job restart, retry and skip, logging and tracing, and resource management.

Overview

In the big picture, Spring Batch is composed of a JobLauncher, JobRepository, Jobs, Steps, ItemReaders, ItemProcessors, and ItemWriters.

A JobLauncher runs a Job with given Job Parameters. Each Job can have multiple Steps. Each Step is typically composed of an ItemReader, ItemProcessor, and ItemWriter. Metadata, or information about the state of each entity, is saved and loaded using the JobRepository.

© Adam L. Davis 2020
A. L. Davis, *Spring Quick Reference Guide*, https://doi.org/10.1007/978-1-4842-6144-6_14

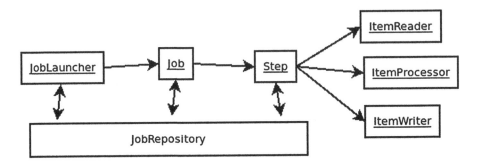

The Example

To demonstrate Spring Batch, we will use an example. In this example, we will use a simple Course definition. Spring Batch will be used to load a CSV file defining courses, convert the values, and save new Course rows to the database.

Build

For simplicity, we'll use Spring Boot (which is covered more fully in the next chapter). Firstly, we'll define a Gradle build with spring-batch, and then we'll cover the Maven build.

Gradle Build

Create a file named build.gradle with the following contents:

```
plugins {
  id 'org.springframework.boot' version
  '2.3.0.RELEASE'                   //1
  id 'io.spring.dependency-management' version '1.0.8.RELEASE'
  id 'java'
}
```

```
group = 'com.example'
version = '0.0.1-SNAPSHOT'
sourceCompatibility = '1.8'
repositories {
  mavenCentral()
}
dependencies {
  implementation 'org.springframework.boot:spring-boot-starter-
  batch' //2
  runtimeOnly 'org.hsqldb:hsqldb'
  testImplementation('org.springframework.boot:spring-boot-
  starter-test')
  {
    exclude group: 'org.junit.vintage', module: 'junit-vintage-
    engine'
  }
  testImplementation 'org.springframework.batch:spring-batch-
  test' //3
}
test {
  useJUnitPlatform() //4
}
```

1. We apply the plugin for Spring Boot and Spring
    dependency management, which allows us to leave
    off versions in the dependencies block.

2. This line defines the spring-boot-starter-batch which
    brings in all the Jars needed for Spring Batch. On the
    next line, we include hsqldb[1] to use as the database.

---

[1]http://hsqldb.org/

3. There's also a library specifically for testing Spring Batch, spring-batch-test.

4. This line tells Gradle to use JUnit 5 for tests.

Maven Build

Create a file named "pom.xml" with the following:

```
<?xml version="1.0" encoding="UTF-8"?>
<project xmlns="http://maven.apache.org/POM/4.0.0"
xmlns:xsi="http://www.w3.org/2001/XMLSchema-instance"
        xsi:schemaLocation="http://maven.apache.org/POM/4.0.0
        https://maven.apache.org/xsd/maven-4.0.0.xsd">
        <modelVersion>4.0.0</modelVersion>
        <parent>
                <groupId>org.springframework.boot</groupId>
                <artifactId>spring-boot-starter-parent</
                artifactId>
                <version>2.3.0.RELEASE</version>
                <relativePath/>
        </parent>
        <groupId>com.example</groupId>
        <artifactId>batch-processing</artifactId>
        <version>0.0.1-SNAPSHOT</version>
        <name>batch-processing</name>
        <description>Demo project for Spring Boot,
        Batch</description>

        <properties>
                <java.version>1.8</java.version>
        </properties>
```

```xml
<dependencies>
    <dependency>
        <groupId>org.springframework.boot
        </groupId>
        <artifactId>spring-boot-starter-batch
        </artifactId>
    </dependency>
    <dependency>
        <groupId>org.hsqldb</groupId>
        <artifactId>hsqldb</artifactId>
        <scope>runtime</scope>
    </dependency>
    <dependency>
        <groupId>org.springframework.boot
        </groupId>
        <artifactId>spring-boot-starter-test
        </artifactId>
        <scope>test</scope>
        <exclusions>
            <exclusion>
            <groupId>org.junit.vintage</groupId>
            <artifactId>junit-vintage-engine
            </artifactId>
            </exclusion>
        </exclusions>
    </dependency>
    <dependency>
        <groupId>org.springframework.batch
        </groupId>
        <artifactId>spring-batch-test</
        artifactId>
```

```
                    <scope>test</scope>
            </dependency>
    </dependencies>
    <build>
            <plugins>
                    <plugin>
                    <groupId>org.springframework.boot
                    </groupId>
                    <artifactId>spring-boot-maven-plugin
                    </artifactId>
                    </plugin>
            </plugins>
    </build>
</project>
```

In addition to the standard Spring Boot Maven build, we include hsqldb (the database), spring-boot-starter-batch, and spring-batch-test.

⚲ Since Spring Batch typically involves an interaction with a database and saves metadata to a database by default, the starter for Spring Batch depends on `spring-boot-starter-jdbc`.

Schema

Since spring-boot-starter-jdbc is on the classpath, and we've included a database (hsqldb), the only thing necessary to initialize our database is to include a file named schema-all.sql under src/main/resources/. Create this file and add the following:

```
DROP TABLE course IF EXISTS;

CREATE TABLE course  (
    course_id BIGINT IDENTITY NOT NULL PRIMARY KEY,
    title VARCHAR(200),
    description VARCHAR(250)
);
```

Course

We define the Course entity as a typical domain class (POJO) with a title and description:

```
public class Course {
        private String title;
        private String description;

        public Course() {
        }
        public Course(String title, String description) {
                this.title = title;
                this.description = description;
        }

        //getters and setters...
        @Override
        public String toString() {
                return "title: " + title + ", description: " +
                description;
        }
}
```

CourseProcessor

Spring Batch provides the ItemProcessor<I,O> interface (I stands for input and O for output) for implementing the logic whenever an entity needs to be modified or processed in some way.

In this case, we define a CourseProcessor that implements ItemProcessor<I,O> that replaces any amount of space with one space and trims any leading or trailing whitespace:

```
import org.slf4j.Logger;
import org.slf4j.LoggerFactory;
import org.springframework.batch.item.ItemProcessor;

public class CourseProcessor implements ItemProcessor<Course,
Course> { //1

  private static final Logger log =
    LoggerFactory.getLogger(CourseProcessor.class);

  @Override
  public Course process(final Course course) throws Exception {
    final String title = course.getTitle()
                                   .replaceAll("\\s+", " ").
                                   trim(); //2
    final String description = course.getDescription()
                                   .replaceAll("\\s+", " ").
                                   trim();
    final Course transformedCourse = new Course(title,
    description);

    log.info("Converting (" + course + ") into (" +
    transformedCourse + ")");
```

```
  return transformedCourse; //3
 }
}
```

1. We declare that CourseProcessor implements the ItemProcessor interface and that both the in and out types are the same, Course. If they were different, the first declared type would declare the type of the parameter to process, and the second type would be the return type.

2. Here, we replace any space with one space using replaceAll (using the regular expression \\s+) in both the title and description. We create a new object so that the Processor is idempotent – it should not modify the input object.

3. Finally, we return the new Course instance from the process method.

BatchConfiguration

Lastly, we define a @Configuration that defines the Step and Job that will be automatically run by Spring Batch. Although we have one Job and one Step in this case, there could be multiple Jobs and one or more Steps per Job. If multiple Jobs exist, you can specify which job or jobs to run as a property (spring.batch.job.names).

Listing 14-1. BatchConfiguration.java

```
import org.springframework.batch.core.Step;
import org.springframework.batch.core.configuration.annotation.*;
import org.springframework.batch.core.configuration.annotation.
JobBuilderFactory;
```

```java
import org.springframework.batch.core.configuration.annotation.
StepBuilderFactory;
import org.springframework.batch.core.launch.support.
RunIdIncrementer;
import org.springframework.batch.item.database.
BeanPropertyItemSqlParameterSourceProvider;
import org.springframework.batch.item.database.
JdbcBatchItemWriter;
import org.springframework.batch.item.database.builder.
JdbcBatchItemWriterBuilder;
import org.springframework.batch.item.file.FlatFileItemReader;
import org.springframework.batch.item.file.builder.
FlatFileItemReaderBuilder;
import org.springframework.batch.item.file.mapping.
BeanWrapperFieldSetMapper;
import org.springframework.beans.factory.annotation.Autowired;
import org.springframework.context.annotation.Bean;
import org.springframework.context.annotation.Configuration;
import org.springframework.core.io.ClassPathResource;

import javax.sql.DataSource;

@Configuration
@EnableBatchProcessing                          //1
public class BatchConfiguration {

    @Autowired
    public JobBuilderFactory jobBuilderFactory;

    @Autowired
    public StepBuilderFactory stepBuilderFactory;
```

```java
@Bean
public FlatFileItemReader<Course> reader() {              //2
    return new FlatFileItemReaderBuilder<Course>()
            .name("personItemReader")
            .resource(new ClassPathResource("sample-
            data.csv"))
            .delimited()
            .names(new String[]{"title", "description"})
            .fieldSetMapper(new BeanWrapperFieldSetMapper
            <Course>() {{
                setTargetType(Course.class);
            }})
            .build();
}

@Bean
public CourseProcessor processor() {
    return new CourseProcessor();
}

@Bean
public JdbcBatchItemWriter<Course> writer(DataSource
dataSource) { //3
    return new JdbcBatchItemWriterBuilder<Course>()
        .itemSqlParameterSourceProvider(new
            BeanPropertyItemSqlParameterSource
            Provider<>())
            .sql("INSERT INTO course (title, description)
            VALUES" +
                " (:title, :description)")
            .dataSource(dataSource)
            .build();
}
```

```
@Bean
public Step readAndSaveStep(JdbcBatchItemWriter<Course>
writer,  //4
                                CourseProcessor processor) {
    return stepBuilderFactory.get("saveStep")
            .<Course, Course>chunk(10)
            .reader(reader())
            .processor(processor)
            .writer(writer)
            .build();
}

@Bean
public Job importCourseJob(JobCompletionListener listener,
Step step) {
    return jobBuilderFactory.get("importCourseJob")      //5
            .incrementer(new RunIdIncrementer())
            .listener(listener)
            .flow(step)
            .end()
            .build();
}
}
```

1. @EnableBatchProcessing enables the auto-
   configuration for Spring Batch, which provides
   the default JobRepository, JobBuilderFactory,
   StepBuilderFactory, and other Spring beans.

2. We create a FlatFileItemReader<T>, which is
   one of the many helper classes provided by Spring
   Batch. Here, we define what file to read from, and

using a `BeanWrapperFieldSetMapper<T>`, we define
what fields to set on the `Course` (using Java Bean
standards).

3. We create a `JdbcBatchItemWriter<T>`, which will
    insert records into our database.

4. Using the `StepBuilderFactory`, we create a step
    which will process in chunks of ten courses (ten at a
    time). Data is processed in chunks for efficiency and
    performance. If any error happens in a chunk, the
    entire chunk is rolled back.

5. We define the Job using the JobBuilderFactory.

For this example, the file, sample-data.csv, might look like the
following (note the extra whitespace which will be removed):

```
Java    11,    Java 11 for beginners
Java    Advanced,  Advanced Java course
Spring    ,    Course for Spring Framework
```

JobExecutionListener

Spring Batch publishes events which can be listened to using
a `JobExecutionListener`. For example, the following class,
`JobCompletionListener`, implements the `afterJob` method and prints out
a message only when the Job has been completed:

```
import org.slf4j.Logger;
import org.slf4j.LoggerFactory;
import org.springframework.batch.core.BatchStatus;
import org.springframework.batch.core.JobExecution;
```

```
import org.springframework.batch.core.listener.
JobExecutionListenerSupport;

import org.springframework.stereotype.Component;

@Component
public class JobCompletionListener extends
JobExecutionListenerSupport {

  private static final Logger log =
          LoggerFactory.getLogger(JobCompletionListener.class);

  @Override
  public void afterJob(JobExecution jobExecution) {
    if (jobExecution.getStatus() == BatchStatus.COMPLETED) {
      log.info("JOB FINISHED!");
    }
  }
}
```

The JobExecutionListenerSupport class implements
JobExecutionListener. This allows us to implement the interface and
only define the afterJob method.

Spring Batch Metadata

Spring Batch can automatically store *metadata* about each batch execution
as an audit record and to help restarts or analyzing errors in postmortems.

The Spring Batch metadata tables closely match the Domain objects
that represent them in Java. For example, JobInstance, JobExecution,
JobParameters, and StepExecution map to BATCH_JOB_INSTANCE,
BATCH_JOB_EXECUTION, BATCH_JOB_EXECUTION_PARAMS, and BATCH_STEP_
EXECUTION, respectively. ExecutionContext maps to both BATCH_JOB_
EXECUTION_CONTEXT and BATCH_STEP_EXECUTION_CONTEXT.

⚷ With Spring Boot, you can ensure this schema is created (tables created) using the following property:

`spring.batch.initialize-schema=always`

By default, it will only create the tables if you are using an embedded database. Likewise, you can keep it from even creating the tables using

`spring.batch.initialize-schema=never`

Spring Retry

Oftentimes, while running a batch process, you might want to automatically *retry*, try the same operation multiple times, if an operation fails. For example, there might be a temporary network glitch, or perhaps a database has a temporary issue. This is such a commonly desired feature; Spring made the *Spring Retry*[2] project for implementing this as a cross-cutting feature – either through AOP or programmatically.

To get started with spring-retry, first include it in the build:

Maven	`<dependency>`
	`<groupId>org.springframework.retry</groupId>`
	`<artifactId>spring-retry</artifactId>`
	`<version>1.3.0</version>`
	`</dependency>`

Gradle	`implementation 'org.springframework.retry:spring-` `retry:jar:1.3.0'`

---

[2]https://github.com/spring-projects/spring-retry

Then, to use the declarative/AOP approach, add the @EnableRetry annotation to one of your Java configuration classes (this tells Spring to scan for the @Retryable annotation):

```
@Configuration
@EnableBatchProcessing
@EnableRetry
public class BatchConfiguration {
```

Or to use Spring Retry in the imperative (programmatic) approach, use the RetryTemplate directly, for example:

```
RetryTemplate template = RetryTemplate.builder()
                              .maxAttempts(3)
                              .fixedBackoff(1000)
                              .retryOn(RemoteAccessException.
                               class)
                              .build();

template.execute(ctx -> {
    // ... some code
});
```

In this example, the executed code will be retried up to three times, only when a RemoteAccessException is thrown, and will back off one second (1000 milliseconds) each time.

Retry Terms

Max-Attempts	Maximum number of retries.
Fixed-Backoff	Time to increase pause between retries (in milliseconds).
Exponential-Backoff	Parameters to increase pause between retries (in milliseconds) exponentially to better solve the issue when the problematic system is down due to oversaturation.
Random-Backoff	It's good to include randomness (from 0% to 200% delay time) to avoid correlation of retries (so a bunch of nodes don't all retry at the same time).

Retryable Annotation

Using the AOP method, you can annotate any method introspected by Spring (on a public method of a Spring bean) with @Retryable (after using @EnableRetry on a configuration class). For example, let's modify our CourseProcessor from earlier to retry up to four times:

```
@Retryable(maxAttempts = 4, backoff =
        @Backoff(random = true, delay = 100))
@Override
public Course process(final Course course) throws Exception {
  // code...
  return transformedCourse;

}
```

Notice how we set the backoff using the @Backoff annotation.

CHAPTER 15

Spring Boot

Spring Boot enables developer productivity by removing the need for tons of boilerplate associated with building a Spring application. It uses conventions and "starter" dependencies, in addition to plain old Spring features like annotation scanning, to greatly simplify developing applications.

At the same time, it is very flexible and gives the developer a lot of agency in deciding what to include, and over time you can modify the configuration as needed.

Introduction to Spring Boot

Spring Boot greatly simplifies creating a Spring-based application or microservice. It simplifies the life of software developers by automatically configuring some things and removing the need to specify versions for every single dependency.

Using Spring Boot, a developer can include many "starter dependencies" which each themselves transitively include many libraries and auto-configuration for the project. This greatly improves the experience of starting and adding to projects. In many cases, Spring Boot includes reasonable default configurations as well. As the project grows, developers can override the defaults and customize the project in many different ways.

© Adam L. Davis 2020
A. L. Davis, *Spring Quick Reference Guide*, https://doi.org/10.1007/978-1-4842-6144-6_15

You can package a web project either as a WAR or as a single JAR file. If using the JAR file method (which is the suggested method), Spring Boot will use an embedded web container, such as Tomcat or Jetty, and include all of the dependencies within the JAR file (known as a "fat jar").

Creating a New Project

There are several ways to start a Spring Boot project:

1. Go to the Spring Initializr[1] website and create a project template from there. There are also tools like Spring Tool Suite that take advantage of the Spring Initializr from your IDE.

2. Create your own Maven-based project.

3. Create your own Gradle-based project.

4. Use the Spring Boot CLI.

You can easily create a new project with any number of Spring Boot starters by going to `https://start.spring.io` in your browser or using the Spring Boot CLI on the command line. It gives you options such as whether to use a Maven or Gradle build, what test framework to use, which language to use (Java, Groovy, or Kotlin), and so on. It then creates the build file, main Application class, a test for a basic Spring Boot application.

---

[1]`https://start.spring.io/`

Spring Boot CLI

You can easily install the Spring Boot CLI using SDKMAN:[2]

```
$ sdk install springboot
$ spring --version
Spring Boot v2.3.0.RELEASE
```

First, use `spring init --list` to see all of the available dependencies:

```
$ spring init -list
```

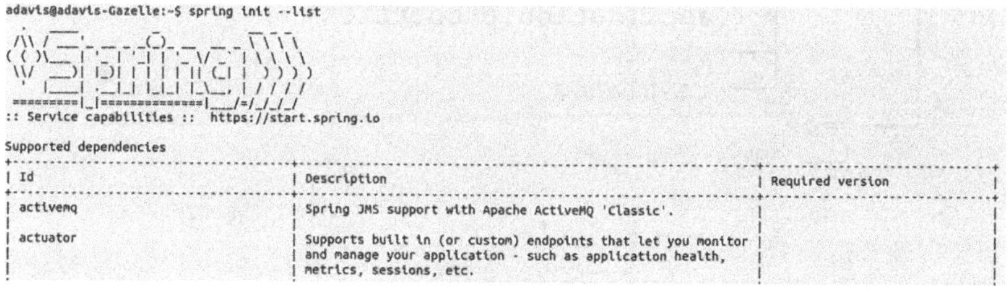

Figure 15-1. *Spring init list: output*

Then, once you have an understanding of which dependencies you need, you can note them using the `spring init` command to create your project; for example:

```
$ spring init -d actuator,web,data-jpa,security my-project
Using service at https://start.spring.io
Project extracted to '/Users/developer/example/my-project'
```

---

[2]https://sdkman.io/

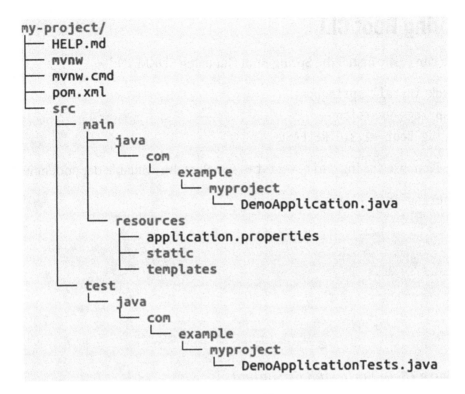

Figure 15-2. *New Spring Boot project file structure*

SpringBootApplication

The @SpringBootApplication annotation tells Spring a number things:

1. To use auto-configuration.

2. To use component scanning. Scanning all packages (starting at the package of the class and all subpackages) for classes annotated with Spring annotations like @Component.

3. This class is a Java-based configuration class (the same as @Configuration), so you can define beans here using the @Bean annotation on a method that returns a bean.

4. It marks the class as the main configuration class of the application (the same as @SpringBootConfiguration) and allows it to be found by Spring Boot tests (marked with @SpringBootTest, which will be covered subsequently).

You must use only one @SpringBootApplication per application.

@Configuration	Marks the class as a Java configuration class that can define beans.	Can have any number.
@SpringBoot Configuration	Same as @Configuration plus it can be found by Spring Boot tests.	Must only have one per application.
@SpringBoot Application	Same as @SpringBootConfiguration plus it enables auto-configuration and component scanning.	Must only have one per application.

Auto-configuration

Spring Boot auto-configuration considers the runtime of your application and automatically configures your application based on many factors, such as libraries on the classpath.

It follows the motto: "If everyone has to do it, then why does everyone have to do it?"

For example, to create a typical MVC web app, you used to need to add a configuration class and multiple dependencies and configure a Tomcat container. With Spring Boot, all you need to add is a dependency and a controller class, and it will automatically add an embedded Tomcat instance.

Configuration files can be defined as properties files, yaml, and other ways. To start with, create a file named "application.properties" under "src/main/resources" and add the following:

```
server.port=8003
app.name=Humble Code
```

This sets the server to run on port 8003 and sets a user-defined property app.name which can be any value.

Enabling Auto-config

Much of the "Magic" behind Spring Boot is auto-configuration – however, you can demystify it once you know how the auto-configuration works.

By including the @EnableAutoConfiguration or @SpringBootApplication annotation on one of your @Configuration classes, you initiate Spring's auto-configuration. This enables Spring's auto-configuration for your whole project. It can do things from creating an embedded database to starting a Tomcat instance.

To locate auto-configuration classes (and other things), Spring Boot checks for the presence of a META-INF/spring.factories file within your published jar. The file should list your configuration classes under the EnableAutoConfiguration key, as shown in the following example:

```
org.springframework.boot.autoconfigure.
EnableAutoConfiguration=\
com.example.libx.autoconfigure.LibXAutoConfiguration,\
com.example.libx.autoconfigure.LibXWebAutoConfiguration
```

Then those auto-configuration classes use annotations
to describe conditions and rules under which they apply. For
example, look at the following example class declaration named
MyReactiveRepositoriesAutoConfiguration:

```
@Configuration
@ConditionalOnClass({ MyClient.class, ReactiveMyRepository.
class })
@ConditionalOnMissingBean({
ReactiveMyRepositoryFactoryBean.class,
ReactiveMyRepositoryConfigurationExtension.class })
@ConditionalOnProperty(
prefix = "spring.data.mydb.reactive-repositories",
name = "enabled", havingValue = "true", matchIfMissing = true)
@Import(MyReactiveRepositoriesAutoConfigureRegistrar.class)
@AutoConfigureAfter(MyReactiveDataAutoConfiguration.class)
public class MyReactiveRepositoriesAutoConfiguration {
```

We'll go through each annotation at a time.

1. @Configuration – Declares this class to be a Spring
   configuration class.

2. @ConditionalOnClass – Tells Spring to only use
   this configuration if these classes are on the runtime
   classpath.

3. @ConditionalOnMissingBean – This configuration
   is only active if Beans of these types do not exist in
   the ApplicationContext.

4. @ConditionalOnProperty – The property spring.
   data.mydb.reactive-repositories.enabled must
   be set to true or missing (matchIfMissing) to invoke
   this configuration.

5. @Import – Imports another configuration class
    which will be processed by Spring.

6. @AutoConfigureAfter – Tells Spring
    to only process this configuration after
    MyReactiveDataAutoConfiguration has already
    been processed.

Excluding Auto-config

You can exclude certain auto-configuration classes by using the exclude
property of the EnableAutoConfiguration annotation, for example:

```
@EnableAutoConfiguration(exclude={DataSourceAutoConfiguration.
class})
public class Application {
/* main method */
}
```

This would stop the DataSourceAutoConfiguration class from being
evaluated regardless of other conditions on it.

You can also exclude auto-configuration classes through a property, for
example, in yaml:

```
spring:
  autoconfigure.exclude:
    org.springframework.boot.autoconfigure.jdbc.
    DataSourceAutoConfiguration
```

Or in your application.properties file:

```
spring.autoconfigure.exclude=\org.springframework.boot.
autoconfigure.jdbc.DataSourceAutoConfiguration
```

Application Properties

By default, Spring Boot will load properties from your classpath from a file named `application.properties` (for standard properties) or `application.yml` (for YAML-formatted properties) plus those files with **-PROFILE_NAME** appended for each active profile.

For example, if you have the TEST profile active, Spring will load the following in this order (later properties can override previous ones):

1. application.properties

2. application.yml

3. application-TEST.properties

4. application-TEST.yml

Overriding Properties

Environment variables can also override any property. Spring automatically converts from an uppercase_underline syntax to property syntax. For example, an environment variable named `SPRING_PROFILES_ACTIVE` will override `spring.profiles.active` from a property file.

The priority order is (earlier entries in this list override later ones)

1. Command-line arguments

2. Properties from `SPRING_APPLICATION_JSON` (inline JSON embedded in an environment variable or system property)

3. Servlet context parameters in `web.xml`

4. JNDI attributes from `java:comp/env`

5. Java System properties (from System. getProperties())

6. Environment variables

7. Profile-specific properties loaded from the
    `application-{profile}.properties` file or a
    similar YAML file

8. Properties loaded from the `application.`
    `properties` file or `application.yml`

Auto Spring AOP

Spring AOP will be auto-configured if included in the classpath. The
configuration will not be activated if you set `spring.aop.auto=false`.

Spring Boot Actuator

Spring Boot Actuator is a subproject of Spring Boot that adds several
production-grade services to an application and will be covered in the next
chapter.

Spring Boot Testing

Spring Boot provides thorough built-in support for testing. For example,
annotating a JUnit 4 test class with `@RunWith(SpringRunner.class)` and
`@SpringBootTest`, we can run integration tests with the entire application
running as follows:

Listing 15-1. BootApplicationTests.java

```
@RunWith(SpringRunner.class)                                        \\1
@SpringBootTest(webEnvironment = WebEnvironment.RANDOM_PORT)\\2
public class BootApplicationTests {
  @Autowired
  private TestRestTemplate testRestTemplate;

  @Test
  public void testFreeMarkerTemplate() {
    ResponseEntity<String> entity = testRestTemplate
        .getForEntity("/", String.class);
    assertThat(entity.getStatusCode()).isEqualTo(HttpStatus.OK);
    assertThat(entity.getBody()).contains("Welcome to");
  }
}
```

1. In a JUnit 4 test, use @RunWith(SpringRunner.class) to enable the Spring test support to autowire fields on the test (use @ExtendWith(SpringExtension.class) instead for JUnit 5 tests).

2. Using @SpringBootTest tells Spring to look for a class annotated with either @SpringBootConfiguration or @SpringBootApplication in the current package or upward and start up an ApplicationContext starting with that configuration. Using "webEnvironment = WebEnvironment.RANDOM_PORT" specifies that the Spring Boot application should pick a random port to run locally on every time the test is run. This helps avoid conflicts with any other running applications. These are the possible values:

Table 15-1. *WebEnvironment enum*

DEFINED_PORT	Creates a web application context with whatever port is configured.
MOCK (the default)	Creates a WebApplicationContext with a mock servlet environment if servlet APIs are on the classpath, a ReactiveWebApplicationContext if Spring WebFlux is on the classpath, or a regular ApplicationContext otherwise.
RANDOM_PORT	Often used in conjunction with a @LocalServerPort injected field on the test (which is set to the HTTP port assigned by Spring).
NONE	Creates an ApplicationContext and sets SpringApplication. setWebApplicationType(WebApplicationType) to WebApplicationType.NONE which is useful to test the server-side logic without the web logic.

This simple test boots up our Spring Boot application and verifies that the root page returns with HTTP OK (200) status code and the body contains the text "Welcome to".

The TestRestTemplate is automatically created and set up to make HTTP requests to the running Spring Boot application.

Spring also provides a @WebMvcTest annotation for creating a test that only instantiates and tests MVC controllers. Any other beans that are required need to be supplied either through your provided configuration or as mocks using the @MockBean annotation, for example:

```
import org.springframework.boot.test.autoconfigure.web.servlet.
WebMvcTest;
import org.springframework.boot.test.mock.mockito.MockBean;
import org.springframework.test.web.servlet.MockMvc;
```

```
@WebMvcTest(CourseController.class) //1
public class WebMockTest {

        @Autowired
        private MockMvc mockMvc;        //2

        @MockBean
        private CourseService service; //3

        // tests...
}
```

1. To test just the one Controller (CourseController), we can use @WebMvcTest and specify that one class (you could specify multiple controllers). Spring will auto-configure the Spring MVC infrastructure just enough to test this one controller. No network I/O actually happens so the test can be run very quickly.

2. WebMvcTest automatically creates an instance of MockMvc which can be used to directly test any Controller which uses Spring MVC (as discussed in Chapter 7).

3. Marking a field with @MockBean tells the spring-test infrastructure to create a mock instance (using mockito) of that interface (CourseService in this case).

CHAPTER 16

Spring Boot Actuator

Spring Boot Actuator is a subproject of Spring Boot that adds several production-grade services to an application such as a health endpoint and metrics.

Default Endpoints

Spring Boot Actuator helps enable common nonfunctional requirements of web services such as health check, configuration, auditing, debugging, and metrics.

By default, Actuator provides many endpoints (mapped at /actuator/* by default). They can be accessed via HTTP or JMX protocols. For example, you can check the default health check endpoint like so:

```
$ curl localhost:8080/actuator/health
{"status":"UP"}
```

Each endpoint can be individually enabled or disabled and typically respond in JSON. Here are all the default endpoints:

- auditevents – Exposes audit event information for the current application. Requires an AuditEventRepository bean

- beans – Displays a complete list of all the Spring beans in your application

- `caches` – Exposes available caches

- `conditions` – Shows the conditions that were evaluated on configuration and auto-configuration classes and the reasons why they did or did not match

- `configprops` – Displays a collated list of all `@ConfigurationProperties`

- `env` – Exposes properties from Spring's Environment

- `flyway` – Shows any Flyway database migrations that have been applied. Requires one or more Flyway beans

- `health` – Shows application health information

- `httptrace` – Displays HTTP trace information (by default, the last 100 HTTP request-response exchanges). Requires an HttpTraceRepository bean

- `info` – Displays arbitrary application info

- `integrationgraph` – Shows the Spring Integration graph. Requires a dependency on spring-integration-core

- `loggers` – Shows and modifies the configuration of loggers in the application

- `liquibase` – Shows any Liquibase database migrations that have been applied. Requires one or more Liquibase beans

- `metrics` – Shows metrics information for the current application

- `mappings` – Displays a collated list of all `@RequestMapping` paths

- `scheduledtasks` – Displays the scheduled tasks in your application

- sessions – Allows retrieval and deletion of user sessions from a Spring Session–backed session store. Requires a Servlet-based web application using Spring Session

- shutdown – Lets the application be gracefully shut down (disabled by default; see the next section for how to enable it)

- threaddump – Performs a thread dump

Configuring Actuator

To enable (or disable) an endpoint, use the management.endpoint.[name].enabled property, for example:

management.endpoint.shutdown.enabled=true

If you want your management endpoints to be served on a different port or path, you can set it using management.server.port and management.endpoints.web.base-path, for example:

management.endpoints.web.base-path=/manage
management.server.port=8070

Keep in mind this will start up a new embedded container (such as Tomcat) to support this.

Exposing Endpoints

By default, most of the endpoints are not exposed. You can specify which endpoints should be exposed via HTTP (web) and which should not using management.endpoints.web.exposure.include, for example (*in application.properties*):

management.endpoints.web.exposure.include=*
management.endpoints.web.exposure.exclude=env,beans

You can also determine which endpoints to expose via JMX, for example, to expose all endpoints except for *beans*:

```
management.endpoints.jmx.exposure.include=*
management.endpoints.jmx.exposure.exclude=beans
management.endpoints.web.exposure.include=*
management.endpoints.web.exposure.exclude=beans
```

Info

You can add custom info exposed by this endpoint by creating a Spring bean which implements the InfoContributor interface. For example, you can use the following InfoContributor which exposes the count of courses from the SimpleCourseRepository:

Listing 16-1. CustomInfoContributor.java

```
package com.apress.springquick.springbootmvc;

import com.apress.spring_quick.jpa.simple.
SimpleCourseRepository;
import org.springframework.boot.actuate.info.Info;
import org.springframework.boot.actuate.info.InfoContributor;
import org.springframework.stereotype.Component;
/**
* Contributes to Actuator's /info end-point with additional info
* (count of courses in this case).
 */
@Component
public class CustomInfoContributor implements InfoContributor {

    final SimpleCourseRepository courseRepository;
```

```
public CustomInfoContributor(SimpleCourseRepository
courseRepository) {
    this.courseRepository = courseRepository;
}

@Override
public void contribute(final Info.Builder builder) {
    builder.withDetail("count_courses", courseRepository.
    count());
}
}
```

Info is served as JSON by default, so the example would produce something like {"count_courses": 0} from an HTTP get at the / actuator/info endpoint.

Health
Auto-configured HealthIndicators

The following HealthIndicators are auto-configured by Spring Boot when appropriate (e.g., CassandraHealthIndicator is only created if a Cassandra database is configured):

Name	Description
CassandraHealthIndicator	Checks that a Cassandra database is up.
CouchbaseHealthIndicator	Checks that a Couchbase cluster is up.
DataSourceHealthIndicator	Checks that a connection to DataSource can be obtained.
DiskSpaceHealthIndicator	Checks for low disk space.

(continued)

Name	Description
ElasticSearchRest HealthIndicator	Checks that an Elasticsearch cluster is up.
HazelcastHealthIndicator	Checks that a Hazelcast server is up.
InfluxDbHealthIndicator	Checks that an InfluxDB server is up.
JmsHealthIndicator	Checks that a JMS broker is up.
LdapHealthIndicator	Checks that an LDAP server is up.
MailHealthIndicator	Checks that a mail server is up.
MongoHealthIndicator	Checks that a Mongo database is up.
Neo4jHealthIndicator	Checks that a Neo4j database is up.
PingHealthIndicator	Always responds with UP.
RabbitHealthIndicator	Checks that a Rabbit server is up.
RedisHealthIndicator	Checks that a Redis server is up.
SolrHealthIndicator	Checks that a Solr server is up.

Custom Health

There are many included health indicators, and you can write your own.
Create your own by implementing the HealthIndicator interface, for
example:

Listing 16-2. MyHealthIndicator.class

```
import org.springframework.boot.actuate.health.Health;
import org.springframework.boot.actuate.health.HealthIndicator;
import org.springframework.stereotype.Component;
@Component
```

```java
public class MyHealthIndicator implements HealthIndicator {
  @Override
  public Health health() {
   int errorCode = check(); // perform some specific health
   check
   if (errorCode != 0) {
     return Health.down().withDetail("Error Code", errorCode).
     build();
   }
   return Health.up().build();
  }
}
```

The possible Health statuses are the following:

Status	Health Method	Meaning
UP	up()	Everything is working.
OUT_OF_SERVICE	outOfService()	Unavailable, perhaps intentionally.
UNKNOWN	unknown()	The status is not known.
DOWN	down()	Something is not working.

If even one Health indicator is not up, its status propagates up to the highest level. In other words, the health endpoint will only return {"status":"UP"} if everything is UP.

Metrics

Spring Boot Actuator provides dependency management and auto-configuration for Micrometer,[1] an application metrics facade that supports numerous monitoring systems. These systems can be very useful in gaining insight into how your application behaves at runtime, either in a staging environment or in production, and enable you to find performance issues early and often.

Micrometer supports many external systems including

- AppOptics

- Atlas

- Datadog

- Dynatrace

- Elastic

- Ganglia

- Graphite

- Humio

- Influx

- JMX

- KairosDB

- New Relic

- Prometheus

- SignalFx

- Simple (in-memory)

---

[1]https://micrometer.io/

- Stackdriver

- StatsD

- Wavefront

Which metrics are available depend on the type of application.

Navigating to /actuator/metrics displays a list of available meter names. You can drill down to view information about a particular meter by providing its name as a selector, for example, /actuator/metrics/jvm. memory.max.

You can also add custom metrics. Inject MeterRegistry into your bean and then use it to add your metric, for example:

Listing 16-3. MyBean.java

```java
import io.micrometer.core.instrument.MeterRegistry;

class MyBean {
  private final List<String> nameList = new ArrayList<>();
  MyBean(final MeterRegistry registry) {
  registry.gaugeCollectionSize("nameList.size",
      Tags.empty(), nameList);
  }
  //...code
}
```

This example creates a Gauge (a value that can go up or down) that tracks the size of the nameList collection. Tags can be used to mark your metric for filtering.

Audit

Spring Boot Actuator has a flexible audit framework that will publish events to an AuditEventRepository. Spring Security automatically publishes authentication events by default. This can be very useful for reporting and to implement a lockout policy based on authentication failures, for example.

Logging

The /actuator/loggers endpoint provides information (in JSON) about the logging configuration of the system and provides a way to modify that configuration at runtime. For each logger, it provides the configuredLevel and effectiveLevel. You can modify the configuredLevel (which typically changes the effectiveLevel as well).

You can request information or a specific logger by using HTTP GET at the /loggers/{name} endpoint, for example:

```
$ curl http://localhost:8081/actuator/loggers/com.apress
{"configuredLevel":null,"effectiveLevel":"INFO"}
```

⚠️ Make sure you have both Actuator configured to expose (as explained earlier in this chapter) and Spring Security configured to allow you access to this endpoint (see Chapter 9).

You can then modify a logger's level at runtime using an HTTP POST with JSON, making sure to set the Content-Type header properly.

```
$ curl -H "Content-Type: application/json" -d "{\"configuredLevel\
":\"DEBUG\"}" http://localhost:8081/actuator/loggers/com.apress
```

You can then request the configuration for that specific logger again to ensure your changes are reflected, for example:

```
$ curl http://localhost:8081/actuator/loggers/com.apress
{"configuredLevel":"DEBUG","effectiveLevel":"DEBUG"}
```

CHAPTER 17

Spring WebFlux

Spring WebFlux is similar to Spring MVC but allows you to use reactive streams and is asynchronous and nonblocking, which, if used correctly, can allow your application to have better performance.

With WebFlux, we can quickly create asynchronous, nonblocking, and event-driven applications using HTTP or WebSocket connections. Spring uses its own Reactive Streams implementation, Reactor[1] (with `Flux<T>` and `Mono<T>`), in many of its APIs. You can use another implementation within your application, such as RxJava if you choose, but project Reactor has the best integration with WebFlux.

By default, a Spring WebFlux application uses an embedded instance of Netty,[2] an asynchronous event-driven application framework, although you can configure it to use an embedded Tomcat, Jetty, or Undertow instead.

In this chapter, we'll take a look at implementing a full project using Spring Boot, WebFlux, and Reactor with a MongoDB persistence layer.

With Spring WebFlux, we can very easily create a nonblocking, asynchronous application with a backing MongoDB, Redis, or Cassandra database or any relational database with a R2DBC driver implemented.

---

[1]https://projectreactor.io/
[2]https://netty.io/

© Adam L. Davis 2020

© Adam L. Davis 2020
A. L. Davis, *Spring Quick Reference Guide*, https://doi.org/10.1007/978-1-4842-6144-6_17

Getting Started

For the purposes of this chapter, we will create a Gradle-build, Java-based Spring Boot project.

Spring Boot is highly customizable, and you can add whichever "starters" you want for your project (web, mail, freemarker, security, etc.). This makes it as lightweight as possible.

We're going to create a WebFlux-based project that uses Spring's Reactor project along with MongoDB[3] to create a fully reactive web application.

The code for this project is available on GitHub at adamldavis/ humblecode.[4]

Gradle Plugin

The basic Gradle build for Spring Boot looks something like the following:

```
plugins
{                                                    //1
  id 'org.springframework.boot' version '2.3.0.RELEASE'
  id 'io.spring.dependency-management' version '1.0.9.RELEASE'
  id 'java'
}
group = 'com.
humblecode'                                          //2
version = '0.0.2-SNAPSHOT'
sourceCompatibility = 11
```

---

[3]www.mongodb.com/

[4]https://github.com/adamldavis/humblecode

```
repositories {
  mavenCentral()
}
dependencies {
  compile('org.springframework.boot:spring-boot-starter-
  webflux')      //3

  compileOnly('org.projectlombok:lombok')                      //4
  compile(
'org.springframework.boot:spring-boot-starter-data-mongodb-
  reactive') //5
  testCompile('org.springframework.boot:spring-boot-starter-
  test')
  testCompile('io.projectreactor:reactor-test')                //6
}
```

1. The first thing you might notice is the lack of
   versions specified; Spring Boot provides those for
   you and ensures that everything is compatible.

2. We specify the groupId and version for the build
   artifact. We also specify the Java source version as 11.
   You don't need to specify the main class. That is
   determined by Spring Boot through annotations.

3. We include the "webflux" starter to enable Spring's
   WebFlux.

4. We're including project lombok here just to simplify
   the model classes. Lombok supplies annotations
   and automatically generates boilerplate code like
   getters and setters based on which annotations are
   used on each class.

5. Here we include the spring-data starter for using reactive MongoDB with Reactor integration.

6. Finally, we include "spring-boot-starter-test" and "reactor-test" to use the test support supplied by Spring.

Keep in mind that in order for the back end to be completely reactive, our integration with the database needs to be asynchronous. This is not possible with every type of database. In this case, we are using MongoDB which supports asynchronous operations.

As of writing, Spring Data provides direct reactive integration for Redis, MongoDB, and Cassandra. You can do this by simply switching "mongodb" for the database you want in the "starter" compile dependency. Spring Data also provided support for R2DBC for relational databases (see Chapter 6 for more).

Tasks

The Spring Boot plugin adds several tasks to the build.

To run the project, run "`gradle bootRun`" (which runs on port 8080 by default). Look at the command-line output to see useful information like which port your application is running on.

When you're ready to deploy, run "`gradle bootRepackage`" which builds a fat jar with everything you need to run the full application in one jar.

SpringBootApplication

The main class is specified by annotating it with @SpringBootApplication. Create a file named DemoApplication.java in the com.example.demo package and put the following:

```
package com.example.demo;

import org.springframework.boot.SpringApplication;
import org.springframework.boot.autoconfigure.
SpringBootApplication;

@SpringBootApplication
public class DemoApplication {
  public static void main(String[] args) {
    SpringApplication.run(DemoApplication.class, args);
  }
  @Bean
  public Service sampleService() {
    return new SampleService(); } //2
}
```

Later on, we can add our own configuration classes to better configure things like Security in our application. For example, here's the beginning of a SecurityConfig class that would enable Spring Security in our application:

```
@EnableWebFluxSecurity
public class SecurityConfig
```

Later on, we'll explore adding security to a WebFlux project.

Our Domain Model

For this section, we will be implementing a very simple website with a RESTful API for online learning. Each course will have a price (in cents), a name, and a list of segments.

We will use the following domain model Course class definition:

```
import lombok.AllArgsConstructor;
import lombok.Data;
import org.springframework.data.annotation.Id;
```

```
import org.springframework.data.mongodb.core.mapping.Document;
import java.util.*;
@Data //1
@AllArgsConstructor
@Document //2
public class Course {
  @Id UUID id = UUID.randomUUID(); //3

  public String name;
  public long price = 2000; // $20.00 is default price

  public final List<Segment> segments = new ArrayList<>();

  public Course(String name) {this.name = name;}

  public void setSegments(List<Segment> segments) {
    this.segments.clear();
    this.segments.addAll(segments);
  }
  // custom toString method
}
```

1. The first two annotations are Lombok annotations.
   @Data tells Lombok to add getters and setters
   for every field, equals and hashCode methods, a
   constructor, and a toString method.[5]

2. The @Document annotation is the spring-data-mongodb
   annotation to declare this class represents a MongoDB
   document.

3. The @Id annotation denotes the id property of this
   document.

---

[5]https://projectlombok.org/features/Data

After installing mongodb, you can start it (on Unix-based systems) with the following command:

```
mongod –dbpath data/ --fork --logpath ~/mongodb/logs/mongodb.log
```

ReactiveMongoRepository

First, we need to create an interface to our back-end database, in this case MongoDB.

Using the `spring-boot-starter-data-mongodb-reactive` dependency that we included, we can simply create a new interface that extends `ReactiveMongoRepository<T,ID>`, and (in addition to the methods already on this interface) Spring will generate the code backing any method we define using a standard naming scheme (as we learned about in Chapter 6). By returning Reactor classes, like `Flux<T>` or `Mono<T>`, these methods will automatically be reactive.

For example, we can create a repository for Courses:

```
public interface CourseRepository extends
    ReactiveMongoRepository<Course, UUID> {            //1
  Flux<Course> findAllByNameLike(String searchString); //2
  Flux<Course> findAllByName(String name);             //3
}
```

1. The first generic type is the type this repository stores (Course) and the second is the type of Course's ID.

2. This method finds all Courses with the names that match the given search String and returns a Flux<Course>.

3.   This method finds all Courses with the given name. If we were sure names are unique, we could have used Mono<Course> findByName(String name).

Simply by extending the ReactiveMongoRepository<T,ID> interface, our repository will have tons of useful methods such as findById, insert, and save all returning Reactor types (Mono<T> or Flux<T>).

Controllers

Next, we need to make a basic controller for rendering our view templates.

Annotate a class with @Controller to create a web controller, for example:

```
@Controller
public class WebController {
  @GetMapping("/hello")
  public String hello() { return "home"; }
}
```

As the preceding method returns the string "home", it would render the corresponding view template.

The GetMapping annotation is identical to using @RequestMapping(path="/hello", method = RequestMethod.GET). It's not reactive yet, we will add that later on in this chapter.

By default, Spring WebFlux uses an embedded Netty instance. Using the embedded container means that container is just another "bean" which makes configuration a lot easier. It can be configured using application.properties and other application configuration files.

Next, we'd like to add some initial data to our repository so there's something to look at. We can accomplish this by adding a method annotated with @PostConstruct that only adds data to the courseRepository when the count is zero:

```java
@PostConstruct
public void setup() {

  courseRepository.count().blockOptional().filter(count ->
  count == 0)
  .ifPresent(it ->
    Flux.just(
      new Course("Beginning Java"),
      new Course("Advanced Java"),
      new Course("Reactive Streams in Java"))
    .doOnNext(c -> System.out.println(c.toString()))
    .flatMap(courseRepository::save)
    .subscribeOn(Schedulers.single())
    .subscribe() // need to do this to actually execute save
  );
}
```

Here the code uses a mix of Java 8's Optional<T> with Reactor. Note that we must call subscribe on a Flux or else it won't ever execute. We accomplish this here by calling subscribe() with no parameters. Since count() returns a Mono<Long>, we call blockOptional() which will block (wait for the Mono to complete) and then use the given value; if it is zero, we then save three Course objects to the courseRepository. For a refresher on using Flux and Mono, please see Chapter 12.

View Templates

In any Spring Boot project, we could use one of many view template renderers. In this case, we include the freemarker spring starter to our build file under dependencies:

```
compile('org.springframework.boot:spring-boot-starter-freemarker')
```

We put our templates under `src/main/resources/templates`. Here's the important part of the file, `home.ftl`:

```
<div class="page-header">
    <h1>Welcome to ${applicationName}!</h1>
</div>
<article id="content" class="jumbotron center"></article>
<script type="application/javascript">
jQuery(document).ready(HC.loadCourses);
</script>
```

This calls the corresponding JavaScript to get the list of Courses from our RestController. The loadCourses function is defined something like the following:

```
jQuery.ajax({method: 'get', url: '/api/courses'}).done( //1
function(data) {
  var list = data;                                        //2
  var ul = jQuery('<ul class="courses btn-group"></ul>');
  list.forEach((crs) => {                                 //3
    ul.append('<li class="btn-link" onclick="HC.loadCourse(\''+
    crs.id+'\'); return false">'
    + crs.name + ': <i>' + crs.price + '</i></li>')
  });
  jQuery('#content').html(ul);                            //4
}
).fail( errorHandler );                                   //5
```

1. First, we call our RESTful API, which we will define later.

2. Since we're using jQuery, it automatically determines the response is JSON and parses the returned data.

3. Using forEach, we build an HTML list to display each Course with a link to load each Course.

4. We update the DOM to include the list we built.

5. Here we specify the error handling function in case anything goes wrong with the HTTP request.

Although we're using jQuery here, we could have chosen any JavaScript library/framework. For Spring Boot, JavaScript files should be stored at src/main/resources/static/js.

RESTful API

By default, Spring encodes data from a @RestController into JSON, so the corresponding CourseController is defined thusly:

Listing 17-1. CourseController.java

```
@RestController
public class CourseController {
    final CourseRepository courseRepository;

    public CourseControl(CourseRepository courseRepository) {
        this.courseRepository = courseRepository;
    }

    @GetMapping("/api/courses")
    public Flux<Course> getCourses() {
        return courseRepository.findAll();
    }
```

```
@GetMapping("/api/courses/{id}")
public Mono<Course> getCourse(@PathVariable("id")
String id) {
        return courseRepository.findById(UUID.
        fromString(id));
    }
}
```

Note how we can return Reactor data types like Flux<T> directly from a RestController since we are using WebFlux. This means that every HTTP request will be nonblocking and use Reactor to determine the threads on which to run your operations.

Note that we are calling the repository directly from the controller in this example. In a production system, it is best practice to add a "service" layer in between the controller and repository to hold the business logic.

Now we have the ability to read Courses, but we also need the ability to save and update them.

Since we're making a RESTful API, we use @PostMapping to handle HTTP POST for saving new entities and @PutMapping to handle PUT for updating.

Here's the save method:

```
@PostMapping(value = "/api/courses",
      consumes = MediaType.APPLICATION_JSON_VALUE)
public Mono<Course> saveCourse(@RequestBody Map<String,
Object> body) {
      Course course = new Course((String) body.get("name"));
      course.price = Long.parseLong(body.get("price").
      toString());

      return courseRepository.insert(course);
}
```

Note that the insert method returns a Reactor Mono<Course>; you may recall, a Mono<T> can only return zero or one instance or fail with an error.

Here's the update method:

```
@PutMapping(value = "/api/courses/{id}",
        consumes = MediaType.APPLICATION_JSON_VALUE)
public Mono<Course> updateCourse(@PathVariable("id") String id,
                                    @RequestBody Map<String,
                                    Object> body) {

  Mono<Course> courseMono = courseRepository.findById(UUID.
  fromString(id));

  return courseMono.flatMap(course -> {
      if (body.containsKey("price")) course.price =
      Long.parseLong(body.get("price").toString());
      if (body.containsKey("name")) course.name =
          (String) body.get("name");
      return courseRepository.save(course);
    });
}
```

Note how we use flatMap here to update the course and return the result of the save method which also returns a Mono<T>. If we had used map, the return type would be Mono<Mono<Course>>. By using flatMap, we "flatten" it to just Mono<Course> which is the return type we want here.

ⓘ For more information on Reactor, see Chapter 12.

223

Further Configuration

In a real application, we will most likely want to override many of the default configurations for our application. For example, we will want to implement custom error handling and security.

First, to customize WebFlux, we add a class that extends WebFluxConfigurationSupport (here it's named WebFluxConfig, but it could be named anything):

```
@EnableWebFlux
public class WebFluxConfig extends WebFluxConfigurationSupport
{

  @Override
  public WebExceptionHandler responseStatusExceptionHandler() {
    return (exchange, ex) -> Mono.create(callback -> {
            exchange.getResponse().setStatusCode(HttpStatus.
            I_AM_A_TEAPOT);
      System.err.println(ex.getMessage());
      callback.success(null);
    });
  }
}
```

Here we override the responseStatusExceptionHandler to set the status code to 418 (I'm a teapot[6]) which is an actual HTTP status code that exists (just for demonstration purposes). There are many methods that you can override to provide your own custom logic.

---

[6]https://en.wikipedia.org/wiki/Hyper_Text_Coffee_Pot_Control_Protocol

Finally, no application would be complete without some form of security. First, make sure to add the spring-security dependency to your build file:

```
compile('org.springframework.boot:spring-boot-starter-security')
```

Next, add a class and annotate it with @EnableWebFluxSecurity and define beans as follows:

```
@EnableWebFluxSecurity //1
public class SecurityConfig {

  @Bean
  public SecurityWebFilterChain
          springSecurityFilterChain(ServerHttpSecurity http) {
    http
      .authorizeExchange()
      .pathMatchers("/api/**", "/css/**", "/js/**", "/
      images/**", "/")
      .permitAll() //2
      .pathMatchers("/user/**").hasAuthority("user") //3
      .and()
      .formLogin();
    return http.build();
  }

  @Bean
  public MapReactiveUserDetailsService
     userDetailsService(@Autowired UserRepository
     userRepository) {
    List<UserDetails> userDetails = new ArrayList<>();
    userDetails.addAll(
          userRepository.findAll().collectList().block());//4
    return new MapReactiveUserDetailsService(userDetails);
  }
}
```

```
@Bean
public PasswordEncoder myPasswordEncoder() { //5
    // never do this in production of course
    return new PasswordEncoder() {/*plaintext encoder*/};
}
}
```

1. This annotation tells Spring Security to secure your WebFlux application.

2. We define what paths are allowed to all users using the ant-pattern where "**" means any directory or directories. This allows everyone access to the main page and static files.

3. Here we make sure that a user must be logged in to reach any path under the "/user/" path.

4. This line converts all Users from the UserRepository into a List. This is then passed to the MapReactiveUserDetailsService which provides users to Spring Security.

5. You must define a PasswordEncoder. Here we define a plaintext encoding just for demo purposes. In a real system, you should use a StandardPasswordEncoder or BCryptPasswordEncoder.

Testing

Spring Boot provides thorough built-in support for testing. For example, annotating a JUnit (4) test class with @RunWith(SpringRunner.class) and @SpringBootTest, we can run integration tests with our entire application running as follows:

```
@RunWith(SpringRunner.class)
@SpringBootTest(webEnvironment = WebEnvironment.RANDOM_PORT)
public class HumblecodeApplicationTests {
  @Autowired
  private TestRestTemplate testRestTemplate;

  @Test
  public void testFreeMarkerTemplate() {
    ResponseEntity<String> entity = testRestTemplate
        .getForEntity("/", String.class);
    assertThat(entity.getStatusCode()).isEqualTo(HttpStatus.OK);
    assertThat(entity.getBody()).contains("Welcome to");
  }
}
```

This simple test boots up our Spring Boot application and verifies that the root page returns with HTTP OK (200) status code and the body contains the text "Welcome to". Using "webEnvironment = WebEnvironment.RANDOM_PORT" specifies that the Spring Boot application should pick a random port to run locally on every time the test is run.

Spring Data R2DBC

R2DBC[7] (Reactive Relational Database Connectivity) is a standard and programming interface for integrating with a relational database such as MySQL in a reactive, nonblocking way.

Although still at an early stage, there are several implementations of drivers including MySQL, H2, Microsoft SQL Server, and PostgreSQL.

R2DBC is covered more fully in Chapter 6.

Netty or Tomcat

By default, Spring WebFlux will use an embedded Netty web container. However, if spring-web is included anywhere on your classpath, your application will run using Tomcat instead. Spring Web pulls in Tomcat as a dependency, and that is the default from auto-configuration.

WebFlux supports running either using Netty (an asynchronous, nonblocking, event-driven network application framework) or the Servlet 3.1 nonblocking standard (using Tomcat or Jetty).

To ensure you run on Netty, you should exclude Tomcat from your dependencies.

WebClient

If you have Spring WebFlux on your classpath, you can also use WebClient to call remote web services. Compared to RestTemplate, this client has a more functional feel and is fully reactive, using Netty as the concurrency engine.

---

[7]https://r2dbc.io/

You can create an instance of WebClient using the builder pattern starting from the static WebClient.builder() method, for example:

```
import org.springframework.web.reactive.function.client.
WebClient;
import org.springframework.http.HttpHeaders;
import org.springframework.http.MediaType;
// later on...
WebClient myWebClient = WebClient.builder()
    .baseUrl("http://localhost:8080")
    .defaultCookie("cookieKey", "cookieValue")
    .defaultHeader(HttpHeaders.CONTENT_TYPE,
                MediaType.APPLICATION_JSON_VALUE)
  .build();
```

This builds a WebClient with a given baseUrl so that all requests made will start with this URL. It also provides a cookie and header to use for every request. There are many more methods to configure the WebClient.[8]

Each request starts with defining the HTTP method, and then you can specify an additional URL path (with or without path variables) and call exchange which returns a Mono<ClientResponse>, for example:

```
// get the Course with ID=1 and print it out:
myWebClient.get()
          .uri("/api/courses/{id}", 1L)
          .exchange()
          .flatMap((ClientResponse response) ->
                    response.bodyToMono(Course.class))
          .subscribe(course -> System.out.println("course = " +
          course));
```

---

[8]https://docs.spring.io/spring-framework/docs/current/javadoc-api/org/
springframework/web/reactive/function/client/WebClient.Builder.html

CHAPTER 18

Spring Cloud

Spring Cloud[1] is an umbrella project composed of several projects related to building cloud-based applications and microservices. These projects include Spring Cloud Netflix, Spring Cloud Config, Spring Cloud Vault, Spring Cloud OpenFeign, Spring Cloud for Amazon Web Services, Spring Cloud Stream, and Spring Cloud Bus. There is way too much to cover in one chapter, so we will cover some of the highlights.

Features

Spring Cloud focuses on providing a good out-of-box experience for typical use cases for cloud-based microservices and an extensibility mechanism to cover others.

- Distributed/versioned configuration
- Service registration and discovery
- Routing
- Service-to-service calls
- Load balancing
- Circuit breakers

---

[1]https://spring.io/projects/spring-cloud

© Adam L. Davis 2020
A. L. Davis, *Spring Quick Reference Guide*, https://doi.org/10.1007/978-1-4842-6144-6_18

- Global locks

- Leadership election and cluster state

- Distributed messaging

Spring Cloud takes a very declarative approach, and often you get a lot of features with just a classpath change and/or an annotation. For example, this example application enables the Eureka discovery client (a client that communicates with a Eureka server to locate services):

Listing 18-1. `DiscoveryApplication.java`

```
@SpringBootApplication
@EnableDiscoveryClient
public class DiscoveryApplication {
  public static void main(String[] args) {
    SpringApplication.run(Application.class, args);
  }
}
```

Getting Started

To get started, you first need to add the spring-cloud-dependencies artifact to your build. For Gradle, this looks like the following:

```
dependencyManagement {
 imports {
  mavenBom "org.springframework.cloud:spring-cloud-
  dependencies:Hoxton.SR6"
 }
}
```

For Maven, it looks like this:

```
<dependencyManagement>
 <dependencies>
  <dependency>
   <groupId>org.springframework.cloud</groupId>
   <artifactId>spring-cloud-dependencies</artifactId>
   <version>Hoxton.SR6</version>
   <type>pom</type>
   <scope>import</scope>
  </dependency>
 </dependencies>
</dependencyManagement>
```

Next, you need to include the spring-cloud-starter and whichever other specific starter(s) you want to use, depending on your needs. For reference, here are the dependency artifacts for Spring Cloud and their descriptions (the groupId is `org.springframework.cloud`):

ArtifactId	Description
spring-cloud-starter	Base starter for Spring Cloud.
spring-cloud-starter-eureka-server	The Eureka discovery server, which is part of Spring Cloud Netflix.
spring-cloud-starter-aws	The starter for Spring Cloud AWS support.
spring-cloud-starter-aws-jdbc	Allows you to easily connect to AWS RDS databases.
spring-cloud-starter-aws-messaging	Supports AWS SQS for messaging.
spring-cloud-starter-config	Supports Cloud configuration solutions.

(*continued*)

ArtifactId	Description
`spring-cloud-starter-consul-config`	Supports Cloud configuration using Consul.
`spring-cloud-starter-gateway`	Provides a simple yet effective way to route to APIs and supply cross-cutting concerns like security, metrics, and resiliency.
`spring-cloud-gcp-starter`	Supports Google Cloud Platform (GCP).
`spring-cloud-gcp-starter-pubsub`	Supports Google Cloud PubSub.
`spring-cloud-gcp-starter-storage`	Supports Google Cloud Storage.
`spring-cloud-starter-netflix-eureka-client`	A REST-based API for Eureka, a discovery client for load balancing and failover.
`spring-cloud-starter-netflix-hystrix`	Circuit breaker with Netflix's Hystrix.
`spring-cloud-starter-netflix-ribbon`	Client-side load balancing with Netflix's Ribbon.
`spring-cloud-starter-netflix-zuul`	Supports intelligent and programmable routing with Zuul.
`spring-cloud-starter-openfeign`	Feign is a REST client that allows you to use JAX-RS or Spring MVC annotations on an interface to define a proxy of a client.
`spring-cloud-starter-vault-config`	Provides client-side support for using Vault, an external secret configuration store from HashiCorp.

(*continued*)

ArtifactId	Description
spring-cloud-starter-zipkin	Supports distributed tracing using Zipkin.
spring-cloud-starter-zookeeper-config	Supports distributed configuration using ZooKeeper.
spring-cloud-stream	Framework for building highly scalable event-driven microservices (requires a message system like RabbitMQ or Kafka).

For example, for spring-cloud-stream, add the following in the Maven pom:

```
<dependency>

  <groupId>org.springframework.cloud</groupId>
  <artifactId>spring-cloud-stream</artifactId>
</dependency>
```

> ⚡ To get started even easier, you could use the Spring Boot CLI as described in Chapter 15.

Spring Cloud Netflix

Spring Cloud Netflix includes support for OSS (Open Source Software) from Netflix, including Eureka, Hystrix, ZooKeeper, and others. Each of these projects serves a different purpose, and they each can be used separately or together.

Eureka is used for cloud discovery, in other words, so that services can easily find each other in a cloud environment without needing to know the exact IP address for each other. Spring makes it very easy to start a Eureka server, for example:

Listing 18-2. DiscoveryServer.java

```
@SpringBootApplication
@EnableEurekaServer
public class DiscoveryServer {
  public static void main(String[] args) {
    SpringApplication.run(Application.class, args);
  }
}
```

Then you can configure the Eureka server as you would using any Spring configuration, for example:

Listing 18-3. application.yml

```
# Configure this Discovery Server
eureka:
  instance:
    hostname: localhost
  client:
    registerWithEureka: false # do not auto-register as client
    fetchRegistry: false
server:
  port: 3000    # where this discovery server is accessible
```

Then, in other Spring Boot applications using @EnableEurekaClient, you can configure them to register with the Eureka server:

```
# Application name
spring:
  application:
    name: SERVICE1
```

```
# Discovery Server Access
eureka:
  client:
    registerWithEureka: true
    fetchRegistry: false
    serviceUrl:
      defaultZone: ${EUREKA_URI:http://localhost:3000/eureka/}
```

You should replace *localhost* with the location of the actual host of the Eureka server depending on your setup or set the EUREKA_URI environment variable at runtime.

EXERCISE: IMPLEMENT A EUREKA SERVER AND CLIENT

Using the preceding instructions, create two applications – one that is a Eureka server, and one is a client service. Perhaps, use an existing Spring Boot application as the client.

Finding a Service

Once you have a Eureka server and an application configured with the Eureka client, there are several ways to "discover" or locate services registered to the Eureka server:

- Using EurekaClient

- Using DiscoveryClient

- Using RestTemplate through the use of Eureka service identifiers in place of the actual URLs

- Using Feign (which is covered later in this chapter)

You can use the more general (not Netflix specific) option, org.
springframework.cloud.client.discovery.DiscoveryClient, which
provides a simple API for discovery clients as shown in the following example:

```
@Autowired
private DiscoveryClient discoveryClient;

public String serviceUrl() {
    List<ServiceInstance> list = discoveryClient.
    getInstances("SERVICE1");
    if (list != null && list.size() > 0 ) {
        return list.get(0).getUri();
    }
    return null;
}
```

The identifier to use is based on the application name; in this case, it
is SERVICE1. In this simple example, we use the URI (Universal Resource
Identifier) of the first service found, if any are found; otherwise, we return
null (URI is more general than URL but has a similar meaning).

EXERCISE: USE THE DISCOVERY CLIENT

Create another Spring Boot application that uses the DiscoveryClient to locate
and call the service you defined earlier. Remember to set the name of each
application using the spring.application.name property.

Spring Cloud Config

Spring Cloud Config includes an abstraction for centralized configuration for cloud-native applications. With the Config Server, you have a central place to manage external properties for applications across all environments. The concepts on both client and server map identically to the Spring Environment and PropertySource abstractions, so they fit very well with Spring applications. The default implementation of the server storage back end uses a git repository to store configuration.

As long as Spring Boot Actuator and Spring Config Client are on the classpath, any Spring Boot application will try to contact a config server on http://localhost:8888, the default value of spring.cloud. config.uri. If you would like to change this default, you can set spring. cloud.config.uri in bootstrap.yml or bootstrap.properties or via system properties or environment variables. You can then add the @ EnableAutoConfiguration annotation, for example:

```
@Configuration
@EnableAutoConfiguration
@RestController
public class Application {

  @Value("${config.name}") // can come from config server
  String name = "";

  //more code...
}
```

To run your own server, use the spring-cloud-config-server dependency and add the @EnableConfigServer annotation on a Java configuration class or on your main @SpringBootApplication annotated class. If you set the property spring.config.name=configserver, the application will run on port 8888 and serve data from a sample repository. Set the spring.cloud.config.server.git.uri property to the location of a git repository (it can start with file: meaning it is a local path on the file system).

Spring Cloud OpenFeign

This project has support for OpenFeign[2] (sometimes referred to as Feign), an abstraction for wrapping REST application messages and building declarative REST clients. Feign creates a dynamic implementation of an interface decorated with JAX-RS or Spring MVC annotations, for example:

```
@SpringBootApplication
@EnableFeignClients                      //1
public class WebApplication {

    public static void main(String[] args) {
        SpringApplication.run(WebApplication.class, args);
    }

    @FeignClient("service1")        //2
    static interface NameService {
        @GetMapping("/")            //3
        public String getName();
    }
}
```

   1. Use the @EnableFeignClients to enable auto-
       configuration of feign clients, one of which we
       define in this class.

---

[2]https://github.com/OpenFeign/feign

2. Here, we annotate the interface with FeignClient
    and give it the name service1. You could also
    add custom configuration, like the following:
    @FeignClient(name = "service1", configuration
    = FooConfiguration.class).

3. For HTTP, we use the @GetMapping annotation
    from Spring MVC to define the path mapped to this
    method. You can use any similar annotation such
    as @RequestMapping or @PostMapping or JAX-RS
    annotations.

In the @FeignClient annotation, the given String value (such as
"service1" seen in the previous example) is a client name, which is used
to create a Ribbon load balancer or Spring Cloud LoadBalancer. You could
instead specify an absolute URL using the url attribute. The load balancer
will discover the physical addresses for the "service1" service at runtime.
If your application is a Eureka client, then it will resolve the service in the
Eureka service registry.

Spring Cloud for AWS

This project has support for AWS (Amazon Web Services[3]), including things
like Spring Messaging API implementation for SQS[4] (Simple Queue Service),
Spring Cache API implementation for ElastiCache,[5] and Automatic JDBC
DataSource creation based on the logical name of an RDS[6] instance.

---

[3]https://aws.amazon.com/
[4]https://aws.amazon.com/sqs/
[5]https://aws.amazon.com/elasticache/
[6]https://aws.amazon.com/rds/

For example, to get started in your application to listen to an AWS SQS messaging queue, you include the `spring-cloud-starter-aws-messaging` dependency in your build file, then use the @MessageMapping annotation like the following:

```
@MessageMapping("logicalQueueName")
private void receiveMessage(Course course,
                           @Header("SenderId") String
                           senderId) {
    // handle message...
}
```

ⓘ For more information, see the Spring documentation for Spring Cloud for AWS.[7]

Spring Cloud Stream

Spring Cloud Stream is similar to Spring Integration's message support but applies only to publishing and consuming messages. Spring Cloud Stream supports a variety of binder implementations such as RabbitMQ, Apache Kafka, and Amazon Kinesis.

The core building blocks of Spring Cloud Stream are

- Destination binders – Components responsible to provide integration with the external messaging systems like RabbitMQ.

- Input and output/producers and consumers – Since Spring Cloud Stream 2.1, there is built-in support for

---

[7]https://spring.io/projects/spring-cloud-aws

using the Java 8 functional interfaces to define sinks (input), sources (output), and processors (both) using `java.util.function.Consumer<T>`, `Supplier<T>`, and `Function<T,R>`, respectively (see the following *EnableBinding* aside for the legacy alternative).

- Message – The canonical data structure used by producers and consumers to communicate with destination binders.

EnableBinding

The legacy Spring Cloud Stream uses the `@EnableBinding` annotation with the value of either Sink, Source, Processor, or your own custom annotated interface. The Sink interface has an input() method, the Source interface has an output() method, and the Processor interface extends both Sink and Source, for example:

```
@EnableBinding(Source.class)
public class TimerSource {
  @Bean
  @InboundChannelAdapter(value = Source.OUTPUT, poller =
    @Poller(fixedDelay = "10", maxMessagesPerPoll = "1"))
  public MessageSource<String> timerMessageSource() {
    return () -> new GenericMessage<>("Hello Spring Cloud
    Stream");
  }
}
```

In this case, it enables polling this method as an output/Source.

```
┌─────────────────────────────────────────────────────┐
│                  INSTALL RABBITMQ                     │
└─────────────────────────────────────────────────────┘
```

On Ubuntu Linux, use the following command:

$ sudo apt install rabbitmq-server

On MacOS, use "brew install rabbitmq", and for other systems, please see the online guide.[8]

Here is the example of *source* semantics using a Supplier<T>:

```
@SpringBootApplication
public static class SourceFromSupplier {
        @Bean

public Supplier<String> source1() {
                return () -> "" + new Date();
        }
        // other beans...
}
```

By default, a simple source like the previous are polled once every second. This can be changed by setting the spring.cloud.stream. poller.fixed-delay property (milliseconds) and the spring.cloud. stream.poller.max-messages-per-poll property (defaults to one).

Here is an example of *sink* semantics using a Consumer<T> (which only prints out the incoming message):

```
        @Bean
        public Consumer<String> sink() {
                return System.out::println;
        }
```

---

[8]www.rabbitmq.com/download.html

Then, configure Spring Cloud Stream to bind to your functions, like the following (in application.yml):

```
spring:
  cloud:
    stream:
      bindings:
        source1-out-0:
          destination: test1
        sink-in-0:
          destination: test1
      function:
        definition: source1;source2;sink
```

If using RabbitMQ, this would create a queue named "test1" at runtime and link both the source and sink to it. The source would be polled every one second by default. Make sure to include a message binding in your build dependencies like "spring-cloud-stream-binder-rabbit" to communicate with RabbitMQ, for example.

Spring Cloud Function is built on top of Project Reactor so you can easily benefit from the reactive programming model while implementing Supplier<T>, Function<T,R>, or Consumer<T> (e.g., by changing your source function to have a return type of Supplier<Flux<Date>>). In this case, polling is not necessary, and you can control the supply of data, for example:

Listing 18-4. FluxSupplierConfiguration.java

```
@SpringBootApplication
public static class FluxSupplierConfiguration {
  @Bean
  public Supplier<Flux<String>> stringSupplier() {
    return () -> Flux.from(emitter -> {
        while (true) {
          try {
```

```
            emitter.onNext("Hello from Supplier");
            Thread.sleep(2000); //sleep two seconds
          } catch (Exception ignore) {}
      }
    });
  }
}
```

BUILD A PAIR OF SPRING CLOUD STREAM APPS

For your final exercise, build two applications that use RabbitMQ: one that
supplies a message and one that prints it out. For the message, use "Hello
from" + new Date(). Use the following dependency for a Maven build (or use
Spring Initializr from Chapter 15):

```
<dependency>
  <groupId>org.springframework.cloud</groupId>
  <artifactId>
  spring-cloud-starter-stream-rabbit</artifactId>
</dependency>
```

See the previous example code for hints. Try the polling method, and then try
the reactive way displayed previously.

Index

A

addInterceptors method, 85
Amazon Web Services
    (AWS), 231, 241
anyPublicOperation
    pointcut, 37
Aspect-oriented programming
    (AOP), 7
  address cross-cutting
    concerns, 33
  advice, 34
  annotations, 38
  bindings, 40
  CGLIB, 33
  @EnableAspectJAutoProxy
    annotation, 35
  JDK, 33
  limitations, 41
  pointcut expressions, 36–39
  terminology, 34
@Autowired, 9–11

B

BeanFactoryPostProcessor
    interface, 14, 15

C

@Configuration, 6, 10
Configuration, DI
  ApplicationContext, 12
  @Component, 10
  component scanning, 12
  import, 13
  Java class, 10
  laziness, 14
  MyService interface, 10
  no-argument
    constructor, 10
  service2 method, 12
  shuts down,
    ApplicationContext, 14
  singleton Bean instance, 10
@Controller annotation, 63
Core Spring
  ApplicationContext, 6
  @Component/@Service, 6
  DI, 5
  IoC, 5
  WebApplicationContext, 6
CourseController, 91
Create, Read, Update, Delete
    (CRUD), 47

Printed in the United States
By Bookmasters